FOOL

FOOL

In Search of Henry VIII's Closest Man

PETER K. ANDERSSON

PRINCETON UNIVERSITY PRESS

PRINCETON & OXFORD

Published by Princeton University Press
41 William Street, Princeton, New Jersey 08540
99 Banbury Road, Oxford OX2 6JX

press.princeton.edu

Library of Congress Cataloging-in-Publication Data

Names: Andersson, Peter K., 1982– author.
Title: Fool : in search of Henry VIII's closest man / Peter K. Andersson.
Description: Princeton : Princeton University Press, [2023] | Includes
     bibliographical references and index.
Identifiers: LCCN 2023008718 (print) | LCCN 2023008719 (ebook) |
     ISBN 9780691250168 (hardback) | ISBN 9780691250632 (ebook)
Subjects: LCSH: Sommers, William, –1560. | Fools and
     jesters—England—Biography. | Henry VIII, King of England,
     1491–1547—Friends and associates. | Great Britain—Courts and
     courtiers. | Great Britain—History—Tudors, 1485–1603—Biography.
Classification: LCC GT3670.5.G7 A64 2023 (print) | LCC GT3670.5.G7
     (ebook) | DDC 792.702/8092 [B]—dc23/eng/20230406
LC record available at https://lccn.loc.gov/2023008718
LC ebook record available at https://lccn.loc.gov/2023008719

British Library Cataloging-in-Publication Data is available

Editorial: Ben Tate, Josh Drake
Production Editorial: Elizabeth Byrd
Jacket: Chris Ferrante
Production: Danielle Amatucci
Publicity: Alyssa Sanford, Charlotte Coyne

Jacket illustration by Joanna Lisowiec
Jacket design by Chris Ferrante

This book has been composed in Arno Pro

Printed on acid-free paper. ∞

Printed in the United States of America

10 9 8 7 6 5 4 3 2 1

The stories we choose not to tell about the Tudors are as revealing as those we do.

I am but a fool.

Contents

Acknowledgments

THE WRITING of this book was facilitated by the kind help of several people, all of whom graciously refrained from pointing out the foolish nature of this venture.

I thank Diarmaidh McCullough, Anu Korhonen, Andrew Zircher, Tracey Sowerby, Elisabet Göransson, and Jaime Goodrich for swift replies to my emails. Comments from my colleagues at the history department of Örebro University in connection with a seminar early in the process were pivotal, and I thank Patrik Lundell, Henric Bagerius, Patrik Winton, Alexander Isacsson, and Björn Horgby for their contributions. Through my contacts with the Nordic network of early modern English scholars, I also received help from Eric Pudney, Anna Swärdh, and Per Sivefors.

Worthy of special mention are Tiffany Stern at the Shakespeare Institute, who guided me in the right direction at a decisive moment in my research; Nadia van Pelt at Delft University of Technology, who provided me with much help and guidance during the final stages of writing; and Gary Vos at the University of Edinburgh, who assisted me in the deciphering of a particularly tricky Tudor secretarial hand.

I would also like to thank Suzannah Lipscomb, who kindly shared with me her own observations and unpublished writings in connection with her project on Tudor fools.

My greatest gratitude, however, goes to Greg Walker at the University of Edinburgh, who made numerous helpful suggestions and comments on the first draft of my manuscript, and to Ben Tate, my editor at Princeton University Press, whose support and encouragement were a constant source of inspiration during the publication process.

Finally, of course, my loves, my life, my purpose—the two Cs.

FOOL

CHAPTER 1

Introduction

THE HISTORY of the English court in the age of the Tudors is rife with intrigue, sectarianism, war, and paranoia. From the tumultuous era of Henry VIII to the successful reign of Elizabeth I, via the boy king Edward VI and Mary Tudor's brief Catholic rule, the political turmoil of the sixteenth century remains a continuous obsession and point of reference in British history. But amid religious and political power struggles, there was one man, completely detached from all this, with whom King Henry spent perhaps more time than any other. A man whose presence at the absolute centre of the corridors of power during the Tudor era today seems like a flagrant anomaly. A man who had constant access to the king's most private quarters and who must have been alone with him daily, but whose importance has been overlooked in favour of politicians, bishops, philosophers, councillors, courtiers, lords, ladies, and other royalty.

His name was William Somer, and he was Henry VIII's fool. The name first appears in court records in 1535, when the king was in his mid-forties, and continues to crop up in documents during the rest of Henry's reign and in those of Edward VI and Mary Tudor. William Somer is even listed as an attendant at the coronation of Queen Elizabeth in 1559. He appears next to Henry in no less than four portraits of him, and the royal accounts list several expensive gifts of clothing to him, from 1535 until as late as November 1558. After his death in June 1559 he began to gain a posthumous reputation as one of the greatest comic figures of the age, often with a tinge of nostalgia for the days before Queen Bess. Thomas Nashe made him a lead character in his only preserved play, *Summer's Last Will and Testament* (1592), and he figures prominently in history plays such as Samuel Rowley's *When You See Me, You Know Me* (1605). When Shakespeare's clown Robert Armin compiled his great chronicle of famous English fools, *Foole upon Foole* (1600), the inclusion of Will Somer was a given, and as late as 1637 a book purporting to tell his life story—usually dismissed as unreliable—was published.

The man who stares back at us from the group portraits with Henry and his children, looming behind the royal figures, is perhaps one of the most mysterious individuals of Tudor history. By all accounts an entertainer and comic, he appears in every depiction gaunt and morose, a curious combination of sage and crofter. According to Robert Armin, Somer had the ability to raise the king's spirits and spent many hours in his private quarters improvising doggerel verse. Could this be the same person whose enigmatic presence in the background of the royal portraits casts such an eerie shadow over the entire painting? When modern historians attempt to describe him, they are never able to resolve the question of whether Somer was a simpleton retained as an amusing "idiot" or a shrewd comedian who could speak freely in front of the king, and often did. The posthumous image of him has been entangled with the real individual, and no one has really fully tried to disentangle them. But achieving that would provide us with a unique window into both the life of the court and fundamental conceptions of humour, humanity, and deviance in the Renaissance.

Judging from the frequency of references to him in sixteenth- and seventeenth-century literature, Will Somer was one of the most famous men of his age. And yet, to this day, no one has attempted to write his biography. Only in recent years have biographies of Henry VIII seen fit to mention Somer at all, reflecting a transition in interest away from the purely political to accounts that also consider things like court culture, mentalities, and the royal household. In the more traditional books on Henry VIII and his times by the likes of John Guy, David Starkey, and J. J. Scarisbrick, a man like Somer never gets a mention. The works that have shaped the public image of the Tudor age in the early twenty-first century—the TV drama series *The Tudors* (2007–2010) and Hilary Mantel's trilogy of novels about Thomas Cromwell (2009–2020)—paint a broad enough picture to include Somer briefly, but the attention is still focused on the monumental men of the age.

We are better served by popular biographers such as Tracy Borman and Alison Weir, who pay due attention to a man who seems to have been an important presence in the king's life, even though the lack of sources and Somer's distance from the rest of court life mean he is present on only a few scattered pages. Weir presents us with a colourful description of the fool's performance: "He had monarch and courtiers in fits of laughter as he thrust his comical face through a gap in the arras; then, with a monkey on his shoulder, he would mince around the room, rolling his eyes. The monkey might perform tricks, and Somers would tell jokes, himself laughing uncontrollably at the punchlines, or mercilessly impersonating those who were the butts of his jests."[1] The scene is truly striking, but Weir cites no sources for this passage, and closer scrutiny of the available evidence reveals that her account is a fictionalised vignette. It is in fact doubtful whether Somer's personality and fooling were of this manner at all, and Weir's characterisation of Somer as a "comedian," although thought-provoking, is not entirely accurate.[2]

A man like Somer is not as important as a Cardinal Wolsey or a Thomas Cromwell if the political life of the era is in focus, which it usually is when historians take an interest in the reign of Henry VIII. And when they don't, it is often Henry's six wives and his role as a husband that attract people's attention. The story of Will Somer sheds light on other things—like how people with a disability or an eccentric turn of mind have been treated in history, the relation between royalty and commoners in the Renaissance, and notions of what constituted comedy in the early modern period. Historians have written interesting books on the history of fools and jesters, revealing their diversity, the philosophy behind employing them, and how folly was perceived and comprehended. But the scattered pieces of evidence on which historians are often forced to rely have meant that the history of the fool is many times contradictory and inconclusive, haunted by combinations of material from different origins and a reproduction of myths or unfounded claims that have been taken as truths. Furthermore, the perspectives and experiences of the fools themselves are almost never considered, and there has been no modern biography of an individual fool.[3]

Why is this? The main reason is simple enough, although also intriguing. Very few court jesters left behind any substantial source material. The comic entertainers who authored pamphlets, jestbooks, or plays were generally clowns of the stage or educated writers. Fools appear to have been antithetical to writing, and those who did write—like Francesillo de Zúñiga, jester to Charles V of Spain, or Zuan Polo, the Italian commedia dell'arte clown—had a discrepant identity.[4] The ideal fool was a man who detested and mocked learning.[5] Many of the clowns in Elizabethan and Jacobean drama at some point in the play either explicitly comment on their distance to learning or in other ways employ comical misinterpretations or mispronunciations of fancy words. The fictional version of Will Somer in Thomas Nashe's *Summer's Last Will and Testament* even exclaims, "I profess myself an open enemy to ink and paper."[6] I am not really interested in the "interior life" of Somer but rather his personality, his behaviour, and how he was viewed and used by the people around him. That, I think, was where he expressed himself, and it was what people noted and remembered of him. The fool lived and worked in the oral and corporeal realm rather than the literate. The jest was an artform that existed when it was performed, and then disappeared—unless it entered into court gossip, then folklore, and subsequently perhaps inspired a writer.

The most foundational aspect of the early modern concept of folly is usually said to be the distinction made between artificial and natural fools. But when studied up close, it seems that all court jesters were natural fools in some way or another—hired because of a physical or intellectual disability, or thanks to their plebeian or rustic character, deemed amusing in its contrasting relation to the conduct of the court. Even the artificial fools, who are sometimes viewed as the equivalent of modern comedians, often came from humble origins and based their humour on simulating stupidity. To have a fool who was a skilled poet or writer, then, would have been a contradiction. Thus, when reading works on fools by John Southworth or Beatrice Otto, you will find that the closest we get to the fools is in household accounts detailing what clothes they wore and in portrait paintings documenting their physical appearance.

There is, then, very scant source material on most court fools, and this is also true of William Somer. He shares with other fools the fate of becoming the subject of mythology and jestbooks after his death, and the tales and portrayals of this posthumous reputation are often used to characterise and describe the fools, even in modern times. A paucity of reliable sources has not deterred historians from writing biographies of men like Charlemagne or even Jesus. The material available to those who undertake such a task mainly consists of chronicles written centuries after the subject's death or accounts written with a hidden agenda. As medieval historian Janet Nelson has pointed out, the "unknowability of another human being" is there "for the biographer of a twentieth-century public figure" just as much as for the biographer of an early medieval king or a Renaissance fool.[7] Historical figures of which merely the myth remains are given biographies frequently, primarily because they are kings and queens, politicians, and military leaders. I sometimes wonder if there would have been biographies of the clown Richard Tarlton, the fool Archie Armstrong, and the actor Richard Burbage—all important men in the history of British entertainment—if they had been kings or serious poets.

Renowned microhistorian Natalie Zemon Davis asserts in her book on the sixteenth-century African diplomat Leo Africanus that she is presenting to the reader a "history of silences," in which she allowed herself greater freedom than most historians for filling the gaps where the sources were silent.[8] In her book, she includes a lot of conjecture and speculation about what her protagonist might have thought or what his motivations could have been. This is a venture which requires, as her reviewer Maxine Berg notes, "extensive contextual research," which permits her to reconstruct the man "out of the persons, places and texts that he could plausibly have encountered; what she writes is a speculative history, a plausible life story."[9] This approach in Davis's work can be traced back to her breakthrough book, *The Return of Martin Guerre* (1983), where she attests in a foreword how in the absence of sufficient source material she endeavoured to uncover "not proofs, but historical possibilities."[10]

This concept has subsequently been elaborated by Finnish historian Hannu Salmi, emphasising the historian's need to consider what possibilities were open to people of the past at a given moment. This applies especially to those people about whom we can learn only very little from the source material. "Just as astrophysicists can determine features about black holes on the basis of inferences based on evidence about that which surrounds them, so also historians can draw inferences about the past even when it no longer offers any direct evidence about its nature."[11] And as a final addition to this conglomerate of methodological approaches, we might append Swedish historian Eva Österberg's words about the possibility of writing "biographies of the silent." Her contention stipulates that although it is not possible to write a full biography of all the twists and turns in a person's life when our knowledge of it is fragmented, we might write "an existential microhistory," which focuses on "a certain chosen path of the individual's life which has proved fateful for their subsequent way of living" or a "condition that has afflicted the individual without their own influence but has nonetheless shaped their life in some way. In order to understand this, the historian constructs a wider context of mentalities, culture or politics."[12]

So how close can we get to a court fool who hasn't left behind any written records? Can we write his biography? *Fool: In Search of Henry VIII's Closest Man* is not a conventional biography, hence its somewhat elusive subtitle. When faced with a type of source material that has been produced after a person's death, the historian often adopts a strategy of studying representations of the person rather than the person themselves, and for such an investigation there would be more than adequate material in this case. But I will here attempt a sort of middle way. Starting in the posthumous legend of the great comic Will Summers (that is how his name was spelled after his death), I will peel away the layers of myth in order to gradually move closer to the man himself. His life's trajectory and mind can be only partly pieced together, so a common biography is out of the question. But what we can attempt is a study of his role and function in the social world of the royal court, which brings us closer to both the individual and perceptions of him. What type of fool was he, and what does this say about fools and early modern views of disability or deviance? What place and role did he have in the court? How did his surroundings treat and view him? How were his actions and utterances spread and quoted, and what attitude towards him does this reveal?

One might object that any fool would do in order to answer these questions—why not choose one who is better documented? Because in Somer we find a combination of the celebrity that Renaissance fools enjoyed as opposed to their medieval counterparts, the proximity of popular humour to the nucleus of power, and an intriguing example of the ambivalent personality of the court fool that transcended the border between natural and artificial. To following generations, Will Somer constituted *the* fool, and his occupation differed from that of Elizabethan clowns such as Richard Tarlton and Will Kemp, who, though hailed as great comics and favoured by royalty, were stage actors and performers of a wholly different slant. And, ironically, although a list of contemporary references to him will fit on the back of a postcard, Somer is an unusually well-documented fool.

But the primary reason for focusing on an individual fool is to finally release the many men and women who were labelled fools during the early modern period from the oppression of terminology. In fact, to the early moderns, terms such as "fool" were not as categorical and clear-cut as they have become in modern historiography, and this can be applied to many epistemological terms. I would like to give just one of all these fools the opportunity to be considered as an individual and thus to see whether after that he remains just a fool or is something more complex and, perhaps also in turn, makes the word "fool" more complex. We live in an age where social categories are perhaps more labelling and constricting than they have ever been. Repeatedly we see how people with an intellectual disability, for instance, are in public only allowed to be representatives of their diagnosis. I therefore consider it relevant to look at an individual beyond categories such as natural and artificial fool without ruminating on which category is the more suitable. The impossibility of the answer, the unreachability of the man himself, is exactly the point.

Our knowledge of the historical figure of the fool owes much to Enid Welsford's pivotal 1935 book on the subject, which in its comprehensiveness and observations has yet to be surpassed. At the same time, it fails to place the fools in their proper historical contexts, and its conclusions are often based on anecdotal or uncorroborated evidence which has contributed to distorting the image of the fool. This partly mythical image has lived on in later works which, although many times insightful, have mingled the fool as a literary archetype with the fools of real life.[13] The first real attempt at writing a history of fools by consulting archival records was made by John Southworth in 1998, resulting in the unearthing of many hitherto unknown facts. His project was marred, however, by misinterpretations and, as has been observed by reviewers, a tendency to reproduce the myths he set out to eschew.[14] Recent works in disability history have shed light on the blurred line between natural and artificial fools in the early modern period.[15] Alice Equestri has shown how all types of fools, whether intellectually disabled or "counterfeit," were viewed according to some notion of disability.[16] A large portion of this school of research relies on Shakespeare's portrayal of fools, and Wes Folkerth has argued, based on the immense diversity of fool types in Shakespeare, that sixteenth-century conceptions of fools and, indirectly, intelligence were flexible and inclusive. Folkerth even speculates how communities responded to local fools according to their individual differences rather than any consistent definition of disability.[17]

The hazy identity of William Somer is his chief characteristic. Southworth is one of only two writers who have attempted to compose a biographical account of him. The other is his biographer in the *Oxford Dictionary of National Biography*, J. R. Mulryne, who compiled a very brief but informative entry.[18] The main theme of both articles is the question of whether Somer was a natural or artificial fool. It is Southworth who is most adamant in claiming that he was an "innocent," referencing the posthumous nature of the witty sayings attributed to him, the fact that he does not appear to have received any wages, and a record of Edward VI appointing a "keeper" for him. This last point is the most decisive for Southworth's conclusion, but it has also been noted that a fool's "keeper" could simply refer to a servant of some sort.[19] Closer inspection indicates that the case is not quite as clear-cut as Southworth has it, even though Somer's status as a great wit and comedian is certainly a later fiction. Mulryne has little choice but to agree with Southworth, who is the only writer to pay Somer any extensive attention. It is curious, however, that a man who was of low intelligence or had learning difficulties should be seen by posterity as a genius comic and one of the greatest wits in history. How did this change come about, if that is the case? Or does the truth lie somewhere in between? Folkerth, Equestri, and other scholars' suggestion that the relationship between natural and artificial folly was more complex invites further study. Perhaps Thomas Nashe knew more than he let on when he had his fictional version of Somer maintain that he was a "fool by nature *and* by art"?[20]

The chapters of this book take the form of concentric circles, slowly closing in on the elusive centre of attention as we proceed. The question is, Will he even be there when we arrive?

The second chapter, "Legend," unravels the posthumous mythology around Somer, allowing us to work our way backwards to arrive at the first mythologisations of him in the years after his death. The third chapter, "Idea," briefly reviews the theoretical perspectives on court life and Renaissance folly that might or might not become useful to us. In the following chapters, we start our journey towards the man himself, first by briefly considering in the fourth chapter what might be concluded about his origins. The fifth chapter, "Place," traces the occurrence of Somer's name in the administrative records of the Tudor court in order to paint a picture both of the court where he worked and of his place in it. The sixth chapter, "Features," examines the contemporary depictions of Somer's appearance in portraits and the possible symbolism of his external characteristics. The next two chapters are concerned with his personality: the seventh chapter is a study of his external traits, as described by those who knew him, and how these traits might have contributed to his role as a fool; the eighth chapter, "Words," surveys contemporary allusions to Somer's sayings and humour in order both to come as close as possible to his comedic talent and mind, and to perceive how the spread of his sayings reveals other courtiers' attitudes toward him. The ninth chapter, "Role," summarises the observations of the two previous chapters by composing a picture of his role at court and how it related to the roles of others. The final chapter, "Legacy," considers Somer's importance, in terms of both his role while alive and his posthumous identity, for the following development of comedy and fools.

Can it even be that it is with him that a process towards modern comedy is begun?

CHAPTER 2

Legend

BY THE seventeenth century, it had become common for comic writers to begin their works by summoning the spirits of past heroes of comedy. "Give room ye Ghosts of Tarlton, Scoggin, Summers," writes an anonymous pamphleteer in 1656, echoing John Taylor's words in a 1613 elegy: "O were my wit inspired with Scoggins vaine, / Or that Wil Summers Ghost had seasd my braine, / Or Tarlton, Lanum, Singer, Kempe, and Pope . . . Or Tilting Archy."[1] By this time, the list of comic legends had grown long. At the forefront were the first clowns of Elizabethan theatre, still within living memory, Richard Tarlton and his successor Will Kemp, but also the roster of comic actors of the late sixteenth century: John Laneham, John Singer, and Thomas Pope. And to the seventeenth-century readership, the name of Archie Armstrong, the then current court jester, was well known. Behind these recent greats were names that had gone from history into opaque folklore but were still mandatory inclusions on this list. Scoggin was said to have been jester to Edward IV and was already a semi- or wholly mythical figure. And then there was the man who by this time virtually everyone referred to as "Will Summers."

Perhaps the most famous appearance of William Somer in any work of literature is a nonappearance. It occurs in one of Shakespeare's last plays, *Henry VIII*, which he cowrote with John Fletcher and was originally staged in 1613. The drama opens with a prologue in which the audience is forewarned of the fool's absence from the plot. Those who have come expecting to see "a merry, bawdy play" and "a fellow / In a long motley coat guarded with yellow, / Will be deceived."[2] The removal of such an expected and beloved character as Henry VIII's fool from a play about Henry VIII evidently had to be commented on and in some way explained. Scholars have seen it as a result of the increasing marginalisation of clown characters from Jacobean drama after 1600, but also in this particular case as a consequence of the popular clown Robert Armin's retirement from the stage.[3] Armin had made it his specialty to impersonate famous fools on stage, and he had both played and written about Will Somer before. Shakespeare and Fletcher's discreet explaining away of Somer is also illustrative of the status of this fool at the turn of the century. The real Somer had been dead for fifty years, yet it is as if he were never more alive than in this period.

When Somer's name is mentioned, both in the early modern period and in modern research and literature, it is primarily the posthumous legend surrounding him that is evoked. Writers of fiction, from Elizabethan playwrights to twentieth-century novelists, have taken the anecdotes and myths disseminated in the decades after his death at face value. On the odd occasions when Somer appears in modern

fiction, he is often the archetypal clever, down-to-earth ob-
server of the crazy events of his age.[4] This depiction is not a
crime, of course, but unfortunately it has occasionally led to
the transmission of this mythological image to works of history. It is nigh on impossible to uncover how the myths
around Somer from the late sixteenth and early seventeenth
centuries came about, but if we want to move closer to the
real man, then it would be relevant to begin with the myths
to discern between typical mythological tropes and peculiar
details that might hail from his own lifetime.

Is it possible to study myths about a historical figure in
order to learn something about the times in which he lived
and how he was viewed by the people who knew him? In folklore studies, the study of myths, particularly about "outlaw
heroes," has revealed the complex dynamics in creating folk
heroes out of historical figures through an oral tradition that
practically obliterates whatever remains of the actual attributes of the protagonist. They are simply inserted into a pre-
existing mythological template that modifies them according
to the characteristics of the hero in the established tale, making the hero more similar to a Robin Hood than they were in
reality.[5] The common view of folklorists is that historical figures that become main characters in oral folklore are simply
appropriated and adapted to the deep-rooted structure of a
popular tradition, and it is often possible to identify basic ancient folktale scenarios in the anecdotes related in early modern jestbooks and broadsides. But there are also sometimes
little tropes and details in the documented stories that do not
fit into the known pattern of oral tradition or folklore, and
which in some cases might be the only possible sources of

information about figures who have not left their mark in any other records. In his analysis of the jest biography of Richard Tarlton, Peter Thomson manages to identify several ingredients in the anecdotes that suggest a basis in reality, or at least an adaptation of the tradition to the protagonist of the tales. Things like stylistic features, the inclusion of seemingly gratuitous information, and uncomfortable qualities like the apparent ill temper of Tarlton contribute in creating a sense of proximity to the man himself.[6]

Principles regarding the portrayal of historical figures in literature differed during the Renaissance, but the modern adherence to fact and truthfulness was generally less important. The view of history as a cyclical process that expressed the same general truths and human qualities over and over again recognised historical actors as representations of general unchanging human types.[7] Such a view might be used to reflect, for instance, on the way humourous anecdotes that circulated in jestbooks could be attributed to different comical personages, since the fool epitomised the same basic archetype regardless of whether they were named Long Meg of Westminster or John Skelton. This was often common practice when it came to ballads and broadsheets, and it was also the case in the use of woodcuts, where the same image of a man might be used to represent wholly different persons.

But how does this rhyme with the notion that the Renaissance constituted what Jacob Burckhardt called "the development of the individual" or what Harold Bloom referred to as "the invention of the human"? Although the idea that the Renaissance contained a flowering of a new type of individualism, common in older historical writing, has long since been a debated issue,[8] the period also saw the publication of biographical and historical works modelled after classical patterns, such as Giorgio Vasari's *Lives of the Artists* and Raphael Holinshed's chronicles. In his history of the biography, Nigel Hamilton singles out Sir Walter Raleigh as a writer who exemplifies the emerging attention to individual minds through his incitement to study the appearances and sayings of past individuals in order to grasp their internal natures.[9] More recognisably biographical works only began to emerge in the late seventeenth and eighteenth centuries, however, first through the experimentations of men like John Aubrey and Thomas Fuller, and then more tangibly in Samuel Johnson and his contemporaries.

This posits the late sixteenth and early seventeenth centuries in a liminal phase where it is particularly difficult to judge the credibility and accuracy of information in literary works on historical figures. This period has been identified as an age of emergent "embodied writing," signifying a growing number of references to actual persons in both literature and theatre, and a "new emphasis on the personal in works of the late Elizabethan era [that] articulated a nascent public sphere." Authors increasingly portrayed themselves in semifictional ways, and their friends or enemies were represented in similarly disguised versions.[10]

The vogue for both Will Somer as a dramatic character and plays about the Tudors began in the 1590s and was about to end when *Henry VIII* was performed. There are indications that two plays that are now lost but which included Somer as a character were performed at the Rose Theatre in 1598 and at the Fortune in 1602, since there are records of a suit for "Wil. Sommers" in Philip Henslowe's diary on these occasions.[11] The second entry was probably in reference to the lost play *The Rising of Cardinal Wolsey* (1601) or its prequel *Cardinal Wolsey* (1602), both of which were at the heart of a fashion for early Tudor history on the London stage around these years.[12] It is possible that the popularity for presenting Somer as a theatrical character began with Thomas Nashe's only preserved play, *Summer's Last Will and Testament*, published in 1600 but probably performed as early as 1592. The high point of Somer's stage career was perhaps Samuel Rowley's drama about Henry VIII, *When You See Me, You Know Me*, first published in 1605. At around the same time, the clown at the Globe Theatre, Robert Armin, who is known to have originally played some of Shakespeare's most iconic fools, published his compendium of famous fools, *Foole upon Foole* (1600), later renamed and expanded as *A Nest of Ninnies* (1608), which of course contained a section on Somer. A coda to this trend might be discerned in the later jest biography of Somer entitled *A Pleasant History of the Life and Death of Will Summers*, first published in 1637 and reprinted in 1676.

So why this interest in the Tudor period and in Will Somer in particular? Of all the pamphlets and plays that might have referred to Somer in this period, four have been preserved to us: Rowley's and Nashe's plays, Armin's work on fools, and the anonymous jest biography. In this chapter, I will examine the depiction of Somer in these four works in order to see what about him was so appealing to this age, and to peel away the layers of mythology that had begun to conceal the real person. Was there any grain of truth in the legendary "Will

Summers," and how had his persona been altered to suit Elizabethan and Jacobean tastes? In addition to these four portrayals, I will also consider the early anonymous play *Misogonus*,
which makes explicit reference to Somer in connection with
the clown of the piece. This drama might be said to constitute
a bridge between Somer's reputation right after his death and
his reputation towards the end of the sixteenth century. But I
want to tell this story backwards, as it were, beginning with
the last main work on Somer and from there gradually peeling
away the layers of folklore to see what, if anything, remains
when the myths have been discarded.

The anonymous pamphlet that constitutes the jest biography
of Will Somer was first published in 1637 and has the full title
*A pleasant History Of the Life and Death of Will Summers. And
how hee came first to be knowne at the Court, and how he came
up to London, and by what meanes hee got to be King Henry the
eights Iester. With the entertainment that his cozen Patch, Cardi-
nall Wolsey's foole, gave him at his Lords house, and how the hogs-
heads of gold were known by this meanes, and were seized on at
his seller in old Fish-street.*[13] The publication is illustrated with
eight woodcuts, two of which are identical. The duplication is
amended in the second edition of 1676, which is shorter as
some of the anecdotes and the final section, entitled "Remarkable passages in King Henry the Eights time, which Will Summers tooke notice of," have been removed. A third edition in
1794 added a frontispiece falsely purporting to be an illustration of "Will Summers's Armour as preserved in the tower of
London."

The text is bookended by a brief philosophical reflection
on folly and an epitaph on Somer. In between, the text con-

sists of a recounting of anecdotes, loosely grouped into sections that vaguely correspond with Somer's perceived career from country boy to Londoner to court fool. It is safe to say, however, that a vast majority of the stories are common anecdotes, and the reference to Somer as their protagonist is purely superficial—they could have been about anybody. Many of the tales are not even about fool characters but simply put Somer in the role of the character who gives the punchline. In one illustrative example, he is hurriedly trying to leave an inn where he has been eating a meal. When asked why, he replies that he was afraid he would be required to pay for eating the chicken that was in one of his eggs. Other tales can be traced to other jestbooks. For example, the tale in which Somer sells sawdust at a market, pretending it is a flea remedy, can be found in *Scoggins Jests* (c. 1540).[14] Another jest about Somer keeping a book of follies committed by other men and King Henry finding his own name in it is found in Thomas Wilson's *The Arte of Rhetorique* (1553), where it is told of the king of Naples' jester. But if one perseveres, the style of the jests changes after a few pages. The stories related to his time as a court fool fall into two groups: stock jests that revolve around a fool character and anecdotes that are slightly more connected to a concrete context. Whereas the former might have been folktales of obscure origins, the latter could be said to be apocryphal myths that might have been circulating as stories about Somer specifically.

One of these appears to be the one alluded to in the book's title, where Somer meets Patch, Cardinal Wolsey's fool, who takes him to his employer's wine cellar to brag, a scene that is illustrated by a woodcut with no claims to likeness (fig. 1). When they open the taps, however, no wine comes out, and

FIGURE 1. Woodcut illustrating the meeting between
"Will Summers" and Patch (presumably on the right).
From *A pleasant History Of the Life and Death
of Will Summers* (1637).

they discover that all the barrels are filled with gold. Upon
hearing of this, the king demands that all the gold be confis-
cated. This story is in fact a retelling of the subplot of Rowley's play *When You See Me, You Know Me* (1605). As punishment, Patch is forced to leave the service of Wolsey and enter
the employment of the king. Since Somer probably entered
the king's service only after the death of Cardinal Wolsey and

the passing of Patch, the story appears to be legend, but Patch and Somer seem to have been well known enough for a pairing to be a popular plot element. As we will see, they had already been paired in earlier accounts. Patch's reluctance to leave his master's employ is also corroborated by George Cavendish's *Life of Cardinal Wolsey*, written some time before the author's death in 1562. Here Wolsey gives his fool to the king for a different reason, but Cavendish stresses the rage with which the unnamed fool reacts to leaving his master.[15]

Of more interest are the passages that do not have the same formulaic nature—for example, the less structured anecdotes or the plain statements that do not try to be jests. Of the latter sort, a passage that is meant to serve as a bridge from the country jests of the first part to the court jests of the second part is worth quoting:

> Many and almost infinite were his Jests which past from him in the Countrey for stupid and simple, others witty and wise, insomuch, it could not be easily ghest to which his constitution was most inclined: but alwaies hee abhorred all nastinesse: keeping himselfe very handsome and cleanly: insomuch, that from the Countrey his fame spread as farre as the Court, and came to the eare of the king, who sent for him to see and talk with him.[16]

Here is introduced a theme that recurs in many discussions of Somer—the difficulty of deciding whether he was a natural or an artificial fool. Some of the stories in this pamphlet present him as a simpleton giving stupid answers to questions, while in others he plays the role of a clever wit, tricking or outwitting his adversaries. The statement could be the author's attempt to explain away the mingling of stories from different sources that when put together portray Somer in contrasting ways. The story of how the king came to hear about this country fool is in line with other apocryphal tales of how famous fools were "discovered" (see chapter 4) and is a bit too neat and concise to hold up.

There are a handful of jests in the book that stand out. One recounts that Somer would sing loudly when walking behind the hearse at funerals. When his father reproves him for this, he says that the priest and the clerk sing only when you pay them, but "I am content to doe it of free-cost." The relative simpleness of this story sets it apart from most of the others. About ten pages into the pamphlet there is a break in the flow of the text, after which come a few anecdotes that likewise appear less structured than the stock jests hitherto recounted. This could indicate that these stories have a different author or perhaps a different origin from the previous section. One of the jests in this section, for instance, is merely a quotation which the author does not try to insert into a formulaic plot: "Being asked by one, why a dog, when he made water still lifted up his legge? he answered, For manners sake, and lest hee should bepisse his stockings." The close affinity between fools and dogs was well established in the early modern period, going back at least as far as Richard Tarlton and his alleged comic battle with one of Queen Elizabeth's lap dogs. It was expressed perhaps most explicitly in Will Kemp's clown role Lance in Shakespeare's early comedy *The Two Gentlemen of Verona*, where he interacts with his dog Crab in several scenes, chastising him for his lack of manners: "When did'st thou see me heave up my leg and make

water against a gentlewoman's farthingale? Did'st thou ever
see me do such a trick?"[17] Even though this short jest about
Somer connects with such a theme, it is nonetheless interesting for its lack of embellishment. Again, we see in a comment
such as this the ambivalent nature of the fool's reply. On the
surface, it sounds like a conscious joke, but it could just as
easily be the topsy-turvy logic of a disabled or eccentric turn
of mind. Or, thirdly, the artificial fool's imitation of such
thinking.

Another intriguing, and lengthier, jest in this section begins with the curious words: "Above all things, Will Summers
could not endure the lye, and if any man told him that hee ly'd,
he would be sure to strike him with the next thing that came
into his hand." Such an introductory characterisation of the
protagonist does not appear elsewhere, and the aggressive,
unstructured nature of this jest calls for attention:

It so happened that hee telling a Tale according to his fashion, one that stood by, and heard him, sayd unto him, Nay
that (William) I hold to bee an arrant lye, at which hee
growing to a pelting chafe, snatcht up a good cudgell, and
came towards him, holding it over his head, and asked him
why he gave him the lye? the other knowing his suddennesse, and that he was but a word and a blow, deny'd his
words, and sayd, he sayd no such thing: Ey but said hee, thou
didst; but said the other, I did not: hee still urg'd it, and the
other deny'd it so long, that at length he brake out, and sayd,
thou lyest in thy throate, and in thy guts, to say that I offered to give thee the lye, at which word he flung away his
cudgell, and sayd, that word hath given me satisfaction: It

was well that thou didst not say I ly'd, for if thou hadst, I would not have left beating thee whilst thou hadst had one whole bone in thy skinne.[18]

The confusing interchange of this anecdote is quite difficult to follow, but the joke is purely on Somer. The heckling bystander calls him a liar, then denies having made such an allegation. "But you did," Somer maintains, and in the end his antagonist tires of being accused and calls Somer a liar for accusing him of lying—a reply with which Somer is content, even though it reiterates the accusation that enraged him in the first place. The story seems to be meant as an illustration of Somer's character and an elaboration of the opening remarks on his dislike of lying. But the repetitive nature of his mounting anger while threatening his heckler with a cudgel appears to allude to Somer's alleged aggressiveness, attested both in the statement that the heckler knew about his "suddennesse" and in Somer's concluding remark. The aggressiveness of the fool occurs in other contemporary tales. It is evident not least in Armin's compendium of fool biographies but not in the section about Somer, who Armin calls "a merry fool." Instead, we see it in his account of Lean Leanard, a provincial fool from Sherwood, whose envious and violent nature is emphasised in the stories about him.[19] Another aggressive fool was Tarlton, whose cruelty is presented in a collection of stories about him that was assembled after his death, titled *Tarlton's Jests*. This jest biography was first printed in 1600 but may have been in circulation before that and is thus much closer to Tarlton's death year in 1588 than Somer's jest biography. Here is recounted, for instance, how Tarlton tricks a physician with a urinal of wine that he pretends is urine. When the physician expresses his concern about the urine, Tarlton cries that it is good, drinks the wine, and then throws the urinal at the physician's head, a seemingly unnecessary addition that has been read as indicative of his status as a figure of carnival licence.[20]

The form of stories such as the brief remark about the dog and the row with the heckler suggests that they circulated not as pieces of formulaic folklore but as recollections of actual events or sayings. On the other hand, considering the pamphlet's late date of publication, there is nothing to allow us to trace these stories back to Somer's own lifetime, and it is perfectly possible that they were originally about someone else, being eventually attached to a known figure of legend as they were passed on from one storyteller to another. This is a common feature of folklore described by folklorists as the tendency of a culture to attach its legends to a "tradition dominant." Although mainly connected to tales of supernatural events that are in time connected to the local dominant supernatural being, this notion could also be applied to historical or legendary individuals.[21]

Of the forty-seven jests assembled in the book, nine or ten cast Somer explicitly in the role of court fool to Henry VIII. In some he is engaging with the king in rhyming contests (the rhymes taken verbatim from Rowley), a few have him commenting wittily on some matter at hand (these could easily be transposed to an entirely different context), and only a few brief paragraphs in the middle of the narrative speak of Somer's arrival at court and first meeting with the king. In conclusion, then, although some of the stories in this book have a more intriguing style and possibly origins than most, there is virtually no verifiable information on Somer himself apart from the fact that he was a court fool. The inclusion of the final "Remarkable passages" from the time of King Henry's reign is merely a heterogeneous list of seemingly unrelated events, from monstrous births to meteorological phenomena and sensational crimes. It seems to have been added to lend credence to what comes before it, but it rather undermines the serious aspirations of the biography.

The closest preceding portrayal of Somer is found in Rowley's aforementioned play *When You See Me, You Know Me*, first printed in 1605 and probably staged the year before.[22] It is clear that this play was familiar to the anonymous author of the jest biography, as the latter reproduces several ingredients from the former. Here Somer, or, once more, "Will Summers," is presented as an out-and-out court wit who comments on most of the business of the drama with erudition and panache. He has full knowledge of the world of politics and international relations and is a staunch antipapist, representing the play's underlying message that Protestantism is the religion of the honest common Englishman. Occasionally, he functions almost as an adviser in the king's dealings with the pope, and at the same time he is completely plugged into the life of the streets, speaking of waterbearers and Billingsgate and how he has been talking to women at a bakehouse. In line with Armin's picture, he is portrayed as the poor man's friend, in one scene bringing petitions from poor prisoners to the king. These qualities certainly suggest an idealised depiction of Somer. Rowley does not seem interested in showing him in a realistic light but rather uses his name and reputation for a characterisation of the fool as a representative of the people in the tale of the Reformation and England's rebellion against Rome.

However, other aspects serve to complicate the picture somewhat. The fury of the king is a recurring motif. At one point Somer refers to the king's "heavy fist" and claims that "he gaue me such a boxe on the eare, that stroke me cleane through three chambers, downe foure paire of staires, fell ore fiue barrels, into the bottome of the seller." This theme is at the forefront of the scenes with Patch, who here is a constant sidekick to Somer and portrayed as more of a natural. Indeed, the king remarks in reference to him, "Who set this nat'rall heere to trouble me?" Somer at one point sends Patch in before the king to have "the first fruits of [his] furie,"[23] and the two fools speak repeatedly of the king's bad temper and how fools are oftentimes the victims of it, adding a somewhat credible dimension to the role. There are also references to Somer receiving a new coat and cap in exchange for his services, which is a known feature of the court fool's benefits, especially for Somer, whose reception of sumptuous gifts of clothing is well documented.

The most prominent part of Somer's presence in this play, however, is his less than amicable relation to the villain of the piece, Cardinal Wolsey. It is here that we first encounter the story of how Somer and Patch accidentally discover the treasures hidden in Wolsey's wine barrels, which seems to be a fictional elaboration of the possibly established notion that Somer was an enemy of the cardinal's. The enmity itself, on the other hand, was, as mentioned, purely the stuff of legend. In addition to this subplot, Somer has a rhyming battle with

Wolsey, the rhymes of which may be found in the 1637 pamphlet.

Rowley's play is conspicuously careless with historical accuracy, bringing together characters that were not alive at the same time and completely garbling the historical chronology. But this was of course not the point of the play, which was rather devised as a tribute to Prince Henry, heir apparent to the crown (who never succeeded, owing to his early death in 1612), evoking the memory of the strong-willed Henry VIII as a prophetic vision of his namesake's future as king.[24] Research has suggested that Rowley was also the author of *The Famous Victories of Henry V*, often cited as the first of the Elizabethan history plays and famous for providing Richard Tarlton with the role of Dericke, which was to become the prototype of the clown in the drama of the Shakespearean era. This has been corroborated by the similarity in style of comedy and characterisation between Dericke and Will Summers in *When You See Me*. It has also been suggested that the rhyming games in which Somer here engages were an attempt to revive the improvised doggerel that Tarlton was famous for.[25] One might take this reasoning a step further and speculate that the characterisation of Somer in this play owes more to the comedy and memory of Tarlton than to the real Somer. If Tarlton, arguably the most infamous and legendary clown of Elizabethan theatre, had been a colleague of Rowley's, then it is reasonable to assume that he would have based the portrayal of another legendary—but more forgotten—comic on him. So we see here how easily the memory of one fool could be transposed to another fool without much alteration in a way that perhaps exemplifies the portrayal of historical figures in a "pre-individualistic" age where they were representatives of a type rather than individuals. By this time, Somer had evaporated from living memory and turned into a legend that could be filled with whatever the author thought suitable. It is not difficult to find Elizabethan writers, such as Thomas Dekker, Robert Greene, and Gabriel Harvey, who invoke the name of Somer as little more than an archetypal fool.

In perhaps the only extensive scholarly commentary on the 1637 jest biography, a brief article from 1952, philologist Charles Mish surprisingly considers the image of Somer that emerges in it as "more credible" than the "rather hasty treatment" he claims Somer is given in Armin's *Foole upon Foole*.[26] This contradicts what most later scholars assert, hastily dismissing the later pamphlet (sometimes seemingly without bothering to read it) in favour of Armin's collected stories. This possibly has to do with the renown of Armin and his closeness to such a prominent figure as Shakespeare, which has meant that Armin is often credited with cocreating the Shakespearean fool figure using his own research into actual fools as a springboard.[27] In the modern edition of this book, H. F. Lippincott considers "Armin as historian" but seems unable to conclude anything definite. He remarks that barely any of the anecdotes he relates about the six fools dealt with in the book can be found elsewhere, and so he is not able to corroborate them, apart from a few very tenuous possible allusions. Armin tries to use the fools he describes as illustrations of six basic fool types, referring to them as a flat fool, a fat fool, a lean fool, a clean fool, a merry fool, and a very fool.

These are not general types, however, and these illustrations are merely a clever way of describing the attributes of the fools he writes about. The Scottish court fool Jemy Camber, for instance, is the fat fool, and Jack Miller, who seems to have been obsessed with cleanliness, is the clean fool, and so on. Will Somer receives perhaps the least informative epithet of merry fool, but his description in some sense stands out from the others in that he does not share their inclination for aggressiveness or compulsive behaviour. Wes Folkerth has noted that Armin's book can be utilised as "an actual sociological casebook, one that helps us to imagine intellectual disability in the early modern context," and goes on to identify the depiction of such symptoms as lack of impulse control and voracious appetite in the fools. Although Folkerth might be taking Armin's narrative at face value, it is often acknowledged that the accounts of the fools in his book are more realistic than those of fools in other jestbooks, and many of the stories appear to convey the behaviour of natural fools and the surrounding community's reaction to it.[28]

Robert Armin's interest in natural fools is well documented. One of the fools of his book, John of the Hospital, a renowned London character, eventually became his role in one of his few authored stage plays, *The Two Maids of Moreclacke* (1609). It is also generally believed that he brought his study of natural fools to the creation of the fool characters in Shakespeare's later plays, including Lavatch in *All's Well That Ends Well*, Feste in *Twelfth Night*, and the fool in *King Lear*.[29] It has also been concluded, however, that Will Somer is the one fool that stands out in his book for not being a natural fool. But this is never claimed by Armin, who begins his section on Somer by referring to him as "the Kings naturall Iester." The chapter on Somer opens, like all the others, with a short poem about him, followed by four extensive anecdotes. In contrast to the 1637 pamphlet, we are treated to a number of concrete biographical claims about Somer. The introductory poem states that he was born in Shropshire, was presented to the king at Greenwich, cheered the king up by rhyming with him, and was "a poore mans friend," using his influence to help people in need. These traits are repeated in the following anecdotes. The first is a story about Somer's uncle visiting him at court. Somer is busy pleading for the life of a man about to be hanged for piracy—"This & many good deedes he did"—after which he receives his uncle and brings him before the king. The uncle laments that a common in his home village has been unlawfully enclosed by a local lord, whereupon Somer persuades the king to revoke this. The story establishes Somer as the poor man's friend but has very little comic business in it. Somer is described as a man who falls asleep very easily—a trait to which we will return—and there is some roundabout business when he meets his uncle. "Are you my uncle?" asks Will, and he repeats the question several times before being convinced.[30] This exchange is reminiscent of a scene in *The Merchant of Venice* where the fool servant Lancelot Gobbo is visited by his blind father. "Seek ye Master Lancelot?" asks the fool repeatedly before being satisfied.

The second story has Somer asking the king three questions to which he himself supplies foolish answers. This story is mirrored in the jest biography, but the questions are different. The style of the questions follows an established pattern, however. They appear to have easy answers, but based on the "foolish wit" of Somer, the answer according to him has a logic of its own. What is it, asks Somer, that "runs terribly roaring through the world till it dyes" despite being born "without life, head, nose, lip or eye"? "Why quoth Will it is a fart."[31] The third story connects Somer with Cardinal Wolsey, as he tricks the cardinal into lending him ten pounds that Somer then gives to the poor. There is no mention of Wolsey's fool Patch, however, and it seems that the unproblematic joining of two fools from different periods done by Rowley might have been out of the question for a writer who claimed to be telling the truth. The final story concerns Somer's rivalry with another, unnamed, jester. To outdo him and seek revenge on him for his popularity, Somer brings "a messe of milke" before the king's party and asks the jester for a spoon. When he is refused, Somer throws the bowl at the jester's face, "in whose beard and head, the bread and milke was thick sowne, and his eyes almost put out."[32] Armin attests that rivalry between fools was a common occurrence, but this was not the first time that Somer had been portrayed as a rival of another fool, and possibly, there was some basis in truth here. This story is also interesting for the sudden aggressiveness that is here ascribed to Somer. Although it is never explicitly stated, as in the jest of Tarlton and the urinal, it is clear from the wording that Somer actually throws the bowl at the other fool's head, since he later gives him a plaster because "he had broke his head."

Somer's bad temper did not single him out from other fools, but it might be read as a vague sign of nonconformity to rules of decorum and, consequently, a deviant mind. The opening words of this last jest are noteworthy, since they refer to the rival jester as "an other artificiall Jester or foole in the Court." Has Armin changed his mind and concluded that Somer was an artificial fool after all, or has he simply forgotten what he wrote a few pages earlier? The inconclusiveness of Somer's state of mind persists. An added concluding remark to the chapter on Somer in the second edition of the book once more clearly states that "hee was simple."[33] The things in Armin's portrait of Somer that stick in the mind are those that seem the least invented—his sleepiness (after rhyming with the king, it is alleged that Somer "layes him downe amongst the Spaniels to sleep") and the description of him in the poem as lean, hollow-eyed, and stooping, which correlates with some of his painted portraits.

Armin's portrait could be said to constitute a watershed in the posthumous depiction of Will Somer, moving us slightly away from the purely fictional and distorted portrayals in Rowley and the jest biography which revolve around established myths, to depictions made in an age when people living might still have remembered him. These earlier depictions are not as moulded by mythological patterns, but instead of being homogeneous because they adhere more strictly to known facts, they are more heterogeneous—as if by moving closer in time to Somer's own age, we are moving farther away from him.

Thomas Nashe's only preserved play, *Summer's Last Will and Testament*, was first published in 1600, but scholars generally agree that it was written and performed while Nashe was staying at his patron Archbishop Whitgift's palace at Croydon (where he was exiled from London due to a plague epidemic).[34] Referred to as a "show" rather than a drama, it is an allegorical pageant about the struggle between personifications of the seasons. Characters with names such as Summer, Autumn, Winter, Christmas, and Backwinter, but also Harvest, Bacchus, and Orion perform their negotiations while delivering lengthy speeches. Thrown into the mixture is "Will Summers," appearing at the start to act as a chorus. He proceeds by commenting on the action throughout the play with a language that contrasts from that of the other roles, not least in its bawdy and low reference points but also in its refreshing humour. On the surface, it seems that this character is present only as a pun on the word "summer," but on closer inspection, it allows Nashe to insert his habitual disparagements, using as his mouthpiece what was evidently a well-known comic figure to the audience.

It is around this time that Somer's name starts to be spelled in the way it commonly appears in later references to him, a spelling that has continued to this day. Instead of "Somer," or, in some cases, "Somers," as it is spelled during his lifetime, it becomes "Summers" or "Sommers." This might have begun with Nashe's pun, although Somer is not used explicitly as connected to the season after this. The discrepant spelling can be read as a sign that Nashe wanted to distinguish the character in his play from the historical figure. Will Summers as he appears here does not show any signs of being presented as a realistic depiction of the actual fool. On the other hand, he introduces himself as "Will Summers' ghost," which suggests both that he has been invoked to impart the spirit of merriment that he as a fool represents in the tradition of a Lord of

Misrule, and that a fictional rendering of Somer himself would run the risk of not being close enough to the original.

Almost all of Summers's soliloquies are filled with references to popular culture, from singing catches and begging to drinking, eating mustard, and playing games. At several points he refers to a "Ned Fool," whom commentators believe to have been the household fool at the palace where the show was originally performed. He repeatedly mentions the harsh treatment of fools, first in the form of mockery: "Such-like foolish beasts are we, who, whilst we are cut, mocked, and flouted at, in every man's common talk, will notwithstanding proceed to shame ourselves to make sport."[35] Then in the form of physical punishment: "My master beat me, my father beat me."[36] In a line that mirrors the gravedigger's reminiscence about Yorick in *Hamlet*, Summers speaks of how Ned Fool once poured beer all over him.[37] The raucous character balances the poetry and pretentiousness of the other roles. One can hardly hope to find references to the real Somer here, but possibly an inkling of a different memory of him than the mythological one conjured up in later texts. He is more nihilistic and unruly than when playing the lead role in a circumscribed anecdote or offering a wry comment in the background of a Jacobean history play. There is an unpredictability in his monologues, which of course reflects the style of the author but is also indicative of a stage clown figure before being standardised into the common theatrical function it would have in later drama.

If one were to identify one characteristic of Somer here that corresponds with the later depiction, it is the reliance on verbal humour in his comedy. Charles Mish remarked that the majority of the jests in the 1637 pamphlet are verbal and based on wordplay, while only very few concern pranks or physical action.[38] Although there are exceptions, as in the quoted story about Somer threatening a man with a cudgel or his alleged singing at funerals, the general image of Somer deviates from that of the Elizabethan clown of theatrical association. The Elizabethan clown was mainly represented by Tarlton and Will Kemp, who were renowned for their dancing skills and acrobatics. Kemp was originally listed in records as a "tumbler" and dancer. Somer stands apart from this tradition of fools being enlisted from the ranks of morris-dancing teams or marketplace tumblers. The close affinity of medieval fools with related occupations such as tumblers or minstrels is absent in all portrayals of Henry VIII's legendary fool.

The earliest known play that makes explicit reference to Will Somer might be said to be detached from the late sixteenth- and early seventeenth-century vogue for Tudor-era drama as it predates the establishment of late-Elizabethan dramatic style. Does this mean that Somer is here invoked in a different way than in the later plays? *Misogonus* exists in manuscript form and constitutes one of the earliest English stage comedies. The manuscript is dated 1577 and has been attributed to both Anthony Rudd and Laurence Johnson, Cambridge men who were later to embark on clerical careers (the latter as a Roman Catholic, ending in his execution for treason in 1582). Most scholars believe it to have been written somewhat earlier, but no earlier than the mid-1560s, and probably around 1571.[39] This puts it much closer to Somer's lifetime, which makes it interesting to dwell on how his name is used in the text.

The plot of *Misogonus*—ostensibly set in ancient Italy but containing references to London and English culture—is rendered slightly confusing, owing to the absence of some sections. It revolves around the titular character, who has an unknown twin who was sent away at birth. Misogonus, having been pampered as a child, has grown into a temperamental man, shown in his violent reactions to other characters' attempts to pacify him in the first part of the play. His father, Philogonus, orders the brother to be brought home, but when the missing twin arrives, Misogonus does not welcome him. Slowly, however, he grows penitent, and the other characters persuade him to reconcile with his father and brother.

A prominent character that is only loosely connected to this turn of events is the household fool Cacurgus, the characterisation of whom lies somewhere between the Vice of earlier morality plays and the servant clown of Shakespearean drama. Cacurgus addresses the audience and indulges in various devices in a way that is similar to that of the clowns in early Shakespeare comedies but is also different from the precursors in ancient Roman comedy. Unlike the slave fools of Plautus and Terence, Cacurgus plays opposing sides against each other instead of being consistently loyal to his master. As the modern editor of the play, E. L. Barber, remarks, he is "much more intent on amusing himself than in helping anyone." The second factor that sets Cacurgus apart from Plautine tradition is that he disguises himself as a natural fool, what Barber describes as "a type unknown in Roman comedy."[40] Cacurgus's mischievous nature follows on from the transformation of the Vice that had occurred in comedies during the 1550s and '60s, like *Ralph Roister Doister* and

Gammer Gurton's Needle, in which clownish characters are portrayed as more farcical and less didactic.[41] Barber proposes that Cacurgus is modelled on the Vice character Nichol Newfangle in Ulpian Fulwell's play *Like Will to Like*, first printed in 1568 but staged and circulated before that, having much impact on university writers in the 1560s.[42]

Already upon his first entrance, Cacurgus is welcomed onstage with the remark: "What is the matter, Will Summer?" Nowhere in the play is it suggested that the character's name is anything other than Cacurgus, wherefore we can only assume that the name is here used generically for a fool. The nature of Cacurgus's entrance makes him appear particularly foolish; he is speaking in a rustic dialect and complaining that he has not received his wages, but is taking some time to get to the point. He acts sheepishly and submissively, fleeing from the other servants who will not pay him his due, and seeks the safety of his master, who lures him with the words "Come me, Will. Come me." But as soon as the other characters have left the stage, Cacurgus turns to the audience with a sudden confidence and impudence, laughing off the gullibility of his superiors, who were taken in by his performance. "I have bepissed my hose," he exclaims. "I laugh at the old fools so heartily. Ha! Ha! Ha!"[43] The simpleminded and docile natural fool was only a pose, and Cacurgus goes on to revel in the way he deceives his employer with this act. But they both have to gain from it. "And proudly, I tell you," he adds, "to every incomer / He brags what a natural his luck was to have."[44] The perpetual hunt for a good natural fool that the aristocracy of the time appears to have been engaged in is here used to imply that one only had to play the fool well enough to gain employment—and perhaps also that this is what some did. One cannot help but wonder, then, whether the name Cacurgus's master gives him is just a synonym of fool or whether it applies to the natural fool specifically.

> What, how with his man's voice he calls for Will Summer,
> "Where have you put him? Bring him hither, you knave."
> And when I am come, my properties he tells:
> How simple, how honest, how faithful, and true;
> And giveth me points and many things else.
> He treateth me thus and makes much ado,
> Persuading himself that I tell him all
> What I can hear his servants to clatter
> Of Misogonus, his son, in kitchen or hall.
> A fool, he think, can neither lie nor flatter.[45]

The name Will Summer is associated with a certain set of characteristics that natural fools were thought to possess: simplicity, honesty, faithfulness, and truth. Believing Cacurgus to be a natural fool, Philogonus thinks him incapable of lying and flattering for the sake of self-advancement, which is exactly what he does. This portrait of the relationship between a natural fool and his employer should probably be read as standard, but the repeated use of the name of a certain fool also suggests that a common image of the relationship between Somer and his employer was circulating at the time the play was written. Might there be a faint trace here of a piece of court or nobility gossip that Will Somer was not so stupid as his master thought he was, and that his master, naively taken in by the fool's pose, lavished him with generous gifts? Maybe a king wants to cling to the idea that there is at least one person who never lies to him.

The analogy between the name Will Summer and the natural fool crops up once more in a later scene, when Cacurgus, intent on tricking his surroundings, turns to the audience with the words: "Ha, Ha! Now will I go play Will Summer again, / And seem as very a goose as I was before."[46] Here the name does not simply denote a fool, as when his superiors use it, but the role of the idiot that he assumes in front of others. In this scene, Philogonus continues to call the fool "Will" or "Will Summers"—never Cacurgus—as if to imply that the fool is actually the famous court fool but that he is someone else when not "performing." Misogonus, on the other hand, has him figured out and reacts with incredulity when he learns that his father has employed Cacurgus as a natural fool ("What? Thou liest, villain. Thou? Be his natural?").[47] Misogonus is the only character who calls him Cacurgus, at one point asking for Will Summer, "the counterfeit fool," whereupon Cacurgus asks him to call him by his Christian name.[48] They mostly seem allied in opposition to Philogonus, who appears to be under the illusion that the fool is actually Will Summer.

Although Misogonus uses the term "counterfeit fool" in the same breath as the name Will Summer, it is quite clear from the plot that Cacurgus counterfeits a natural fool and that the name is closely associated with the identity of the natural fool. The natural fool is here presented as a truth teller who is incapable of lying and therefore tells his master everything without censorship. Rather than being portrayed as having the licence to speak freely or say anything he likes to his master, in the way that fools were depicted in literature from Erasmus to Shakespeare, the fool comes across as a confidante of his master, one who lets him in on the gossip around him rather than saying blunt things in order to puncture his self-importance. The presumed incapacity for lying might have been the main appeal in keeping a natural fool.

We have now moved back in time, from the mid-seventeenth century, when the legend of Somer had all but consumed what remained of the truth about him, to a time roughly a decade after his death, when Somer's name was invoked to connote a fool that eluded the distinction between natural and artificial. By peeling away the layers of myth that gradually obscured the real figure, we might arrive at something that differs from the legend even though there is no way of telling whether it is the truth. I have in this chapter adopted a slightly unmethodical method of extracting those parts of the mythology that appear to have little purpose for the telling of the story, or claims and scenes that tend to recur in various places, specifically connected to Somer rather than being tales that can be appended to any jester. It seems, for instance, that the memory of Will Somer became intertwined with the memories of other men who became mythological figures of fun in later print culture, especially John Skelton, who was tutor to Henry VIII and who became the protagonist of numerous antipapist jests, and, as mentioned, John Scoggin, alleged jester to Edward IV in the fifteenth century.[49]

More manifestly, the myth of Somer appears to have acquired new blood from the posthumous reputation of the later stage clown Richard Tarlton by the beginning of the seventeenth century. This is particularly apparent in the scene that Alison Weir and Tracy Borman recount in their respective books about how Somer made his audience roar with laughter when peeping out with his head in between two hangings before entering and making funny faces and rolling his eyes. This scene comes directly from the 1637 jest biography, but Armin also in passing refers to Somer coming out from behind an arras. This comic turn of sticking one's head into the scene and making the audience lose control simply from seeing the fool's silly face was something that Tarlton was known for.[50] Several references to him performing this simple trick can be found in literature from the decades after his death, and although these might also be apocryphal, the writers mentioning it were more closely connected to Tarlton. It simply appears that the trick became so typical of a fool's entrance that it eventually attached itself to Somer as well, in his role as tradition dominant within the folklore. As Katherine Duncan-Jones remarks in her work on Tarlton, it was a device that a later comic such as Eric Morecambe also adopted.[51]

In the late sixteenth century, Somer's name crops up occasionally as a byword for folly. Ulpian Fulwell uses the phrase "as wise as Will Summer" in 1579.[52] In a tract of 1566, theologian Thomas Stapleton, when polemicising against his adversaries, contrasts the folly of the fool with the learning of scholars: "You dispute . . . as if an infidell would dispute against S. Lukes ghospell. . . . Will Somer, if he liued, by such meanes might dispute with the best Scholer in Englande."[53] Only rarely is Somer characterised more explicitly. In 1593, Gabriel Harvey refers to him as "the chollericke foole," which might connect to a tradition about a bad-tempered Somer that is less mythical than others.[54] As we shall see, there were several references to Somer in published literature also from the time when he was still alive, albeit mainly from the last years of his life. He was evidently a well-known figure, at least among London writers and prominent publicists, but few seem to have been very close to him or met him themselves. Unlike Tarlton and other more public comics, who were occasionally spoken of in a way that clearly signalled a personal acquaintance with the writer, Somer—perhaps obviously, being a court fool—was a man of whom people had heard but who few had the chance to meet, therefore unsurprisingly giving rise to myths and rumour. H. F. Lippincott has remarked that Somer's name had become a household word, but the tradition surrounding him was so vague that it could be filled with any characteristics.[55]

Having worked our way through this tangle of mythology, I have tried to keep an eye open for things that ring true, that do not strike one as typical ingredients of fairytales. Thus, from our close examination of several works, we can distinguish a number of traits that are either recurring or do not serve any immediate purpose in the narrative:

- He had a bad temper
- He often fell asleep
- He endured physical punishment
- He slept with the spaniels
- He was not a physical comedian
- He was a natural fool or pretended to be one

Some of these appear more credible than others, but the less credible ones, such as the rhyming games or his charity, are repeated in more than one source and so should be examined before being dismissed. It is not a long list, I grant you, and one might wonder whether this exercise was worthwhile if we want to get close to the image of the real Will Somer rather than the legend surrounding him. But the legend has overshadowed him so much that I feel it is necessary to see what in it should be discarded and what should be kept before we carry on. From this, we see above all else how the image of Will Somer still being reproduced by serious historians is heavily reliant on the legend. Instead of simply reproducing the legend, picking it apart uncovers details that will help us learn something more substantial about the outlook and role of a court fool in the Tudor age.

CHAPTER 3

Idea

ON THE face of it, the attitudes toward and treatment of fools in the Renaissance—both household fools and intellectually disabled individuals in society—are highly contradictory. On the one hand, household and court fools were commonly laughed at and even beaten; on the other, they were seen to represent a closeness to both nature and God. Trying to resolve this dilemma in the intermittently conflicting and heterogeneous literature on early modern fools and folly is not an easy task.

The Renaissance culture of folly is a contested issue, to say the least. In a pivotal article in 2010, Paromita Chakravarti polemicises against the overreliance on humanist literature and drama as primary sources for the historical picture of the fool in the early modern period. This lopsided view produced, she contends, the notion that a positive view of and logical place for the fool in the Renaissance were succeeded by increasing confinement and exclusion of fools in a subsequent "Age of Reason." Such a concise historical progression, she argues, fed into numerous influential works on folly, madness, and related issues by Michel Foucault, Anton Zijderveld, Enid Welsford, George Rosen, and others that created a too orderly picture of the early modern period.[1] She might have referred also to the influential works in humour history by Mikhail Bakhtin, Peter Burke, and Keith Thomas, in whose depictions this narrative of a development from licentious Renaissance carnival to civilised Enlightenment wit similarly lurks in the background, although they have been formative not least in drawing scholarly attention to these topics.[2] Chakravarti's remedy was to move to "medico-legal and politico-theological debates on 'naturals', 'monsters' and natives,"[3] stressing a continuity between Renaissance and Enlightenment thinking in the debates on whether fools, monsters, and non-European natives should be considered human. The picture she arrives at points to how discussions of natural fools, primitive peoples, and "monsters" from the Renaissance to the Enlightenment were united by a view of them as representatives of a precivilised "infancy of mankind," linking their mental state to that of children.

Ironically, Chakravarti's article has mainly been referenced in literary studies, especially on fools in Shakespeare. Later works on ideas of folly and idiocy in the Middle Ages and early modern period have not connected their findings to her ambitions, despite assuming similar perspectives. Irina Metzler examines discourses of folly and idiocy in medieval legal, medical, and theological texts, moving into the Renaissance period, and she stresses the fluidity of norms and labels of folly. There was no attempt to arrive at any precise definitions of mental states in the way that modern science does. Metzler points to the repeatedly positive charging of natural fools in medieval religious literature, aligning them with children in their "inability to be sinful." She remarks how medical texts were not as interested in fools because natural folly was not considered treatable, but theological and philosophical texts were, since there it posed "interesting academic problems for analyses of what it is to be human, and how deviations from the norm can be explained as part of divine creation."[4] At the same time, however, she notes how household fools were often subjected to physical punishment. "Fools, like children and animals, had to be chastised, and since their verbal skills were deficient, the chosen means was corporal punishment."[5]

The more negative views of folly in the Renaissance period are often associated with the German humanist writer Sebastian Brant's enormously successful book *The Ship of Fools* (1494), which was translated into several languages, including English in 1509. Brant uses the image of the fool as a symbol of the vices and moral weaknesses of humans and asserts that all the world's ills derived from human folly, which he connects to selfishness, shortsightedness, and frivolity. This one-sided view was later adjusted by Erasmus of Rotterdam in his *Praise of Folly* (1511), which calls attention to more positive types of folly, such as the folly of love, bodily pleasures, and the ecstatic madness that moves a person beyond everyday matters and into a mystical association with Christ. But, as noted by Erik Midelfort, Erasmus is so focused on the moral and philosophical dimensions of folly that he had little to say about everyday perceptions of and attitudes toward folly or about natural fools.[6] Midelfort devotes a chapter of his book on madness in sixteenth-century Germany to the culture of fools and court fools and provides a few vital observations on the role and conditions of fools in real life: Firstly, that court fools became popular because they, with their simple and naive ways, "defied the increasingly delicate standards of courtesy, or restrained courtly behavior," a view that corresponds with Norbert Elias's classic, and contested, notion of the civilising process after the Middle Ages. Secondly, Midelfort underlines that the idea of the "wise fool" with licence to speak freely in front of the king is a literary construction that has little to do with reality. He mentions the common medical theory of the time that presumed princes were prone to dangerous melancholy which had to be relieved. Fools, then, were "little better than slaves or pets" which could be "beaten, manipulated, coddled, and laughed at," and they probably "preferred the abuse they received at court to the neglect and abuse they might as easily have received on the road or at home in the village."[7]

Midelfort's image agrees with the contrast between humanist thinking and the rough treatment of fools in real life that Chakravarti propounds. But the picture still doesn't quite add up, does it? Were the sympathetic ideas of humanists and theologians so detached from everyday life that even those who wrote compassionately about fools could turn around and viciously beat them? Chakravarti mentions an incident reported by Thomas More in one of his letters, in which he had the local constables seize a mentally ill man who had caused a disturbance at his parish church. He describes with some relish how the constables tied the madman to a tree in front of "the whole town" and whipped him with rods until he was weary.[8] Similarly, Pamela Allen Brown has introduced the concept of "Bad Fun" as a descriptor of the type of cruel, violent sense of humour often found in the early modern period. Brown notes how people saw humour in torture, executions, bear baitings, caged madmen, and deformed children and also mentions the sometimes cruel treatment of household fools.[9] The concept that she proposes is rather crude, lumping together various forms of entertainment and contexts under one heading, but the cruelty towards fools in the early modern period is referred to often enough for it to be considered a fact, as we shall see.

A more comprehensive analysis of the treatment of and attitudes toward fools is provided by Finnish historian Anu Korhonen, who considers the early modern culture of violence and cruelty alongside the culture of trickery and conceptions of the body. Citing Peter Burke, she remarks how jests and practical jokes were customarily seen from the perspective of the joker and the bystander rather than the victim, who was frequently humiliated in violent ways. She also refers to A. J. Finch's work on the nature of violence in the Middle Ages, which stresses the relative rarity in daily life of bloody violence and mutilations compared with fistfights and blows. Consequently, the tolerance for violence of this sort was presumably greater than in the modern age, and the violence inflicted on the fool was merely amusing since fools were not supposed to inspire pity.[10] While the artificial fool was funny in his insightful and satiric comments, the natural fool excited laughter through his inability to function as other people could. "The natural fool," concludes Korhonen, "was comic through the definitions and interpretations others applied in observing him."[11]

This perception of the fool contrasts with Metzler's focus on the sympathetic view of the fool in medieval theology and philosophy. In Christian practice, the idea that fools were symbols of unworldly wisdom stemmed from the writings of Saint Paul and was highly influential in medieval monastic life. At the same time, the Old Testament asserted that madness was divine punishment for sin. Korhonen finds, however, that medieval ideas of holy fools and the fool's incapacity to sin were not very influential in English Renaissance culture. Instead, an opposing religious interpretation of folly had more sway: "folly as alienation from God: the fool turned his back on God's grace and became the ultimate symbol of the sinning human being."[12] The fool, in other words, was a walking contradiction as far as theology was concerned. On the one hand, he was innocent and thus incapable of sin. On the other, he was ignorant and stupid and thus steeped in sin.[13] The most common biblical saying quoted in reference to fools was the psalm line "The foole hathe said in his heart, there is no God."[14] In medieval psalters, this psalm was usually illustrated with an illumination of King David next to a fool. In Henry VIII's psalter, there is an image of Henry together with Will Somer.

Thomas More's Utopians "have singular delite & pleasure in foles," and More insists that to laugh at a fool and to take pleasure in foolishness "dothe muche good to the fooles."[15] In opposition to the modern notion that laughing at a fool is humiliating and insulting, More seems to tap into a belief that the fool benefits from the laughter just as much as the person who laughs. Sarah Carpenter interprets this as an indication that laughing at a natural fool was not considered cruel but rather the opposite, since it was seen as separate from the mockery of laughing *at* a deformed or disabled person. Carpenter, in line with other scholars writing on medieval views of disability, notes how contemporaries often compared it to the joyous and affectionate response to the simplicity and innocence of children. Citing Somer's ability to cheer up the king as an example, Carpenter concludes that natural fools primarily "lighten[ed] care with harmless fun, especially for those who themselves carried heavy responsibilities." However, Carpenter also acknowledges the curious mixture of affection and aggression in the relationship between fools and their employers, which attests to the coexistence of grace and sinfulness in the fool.[16]

The opposing views on fools are rendered more complicated, however, when we consider how a differing opinion of types of fools emerged towards the end of the Middle Ages. As both Sandra Billington and John Southworth assert in their histories of the fool, a growing hostility towards artificial fools, or sane people who made a living mimicking idiots, led to a separation between the fool and the Vice, the stock character of the morality plays that became a precursor to the clown of Elizabethan drama.[17] It is also difficult to decide the ratio of natural to artificial fools in the Middle Ages and Renaissance, not least since entertainers who feigned foolishness might also have been other types of performers and thus perhaps called jugglers or minstrels. Some scholars suggest that artificial fools became more common later, in the seventeenth century or so.[18] This has been dismissed by Metzler, who has found records of skilled fools in early medieval records, even suggesting that the artificial type came first.[19] In many ways, we might consider artificial fools as something else entirely since their lot in life and their relation to the role of fool must oftentimes have been different, but there are also examples of artificial fools whose acts resembled the behaviour of naturals. In a fascinating article on the political function of fools at sixteenth-century courts, Nadia van Pelt examines an account of a fool in the retinue of the Spanish ambassador at Katherine of Aragon's deathbed. Analysing this unnamed fool's presence alongside other references to Spanish court fools, van Pelt maintains that fools in Spanish courts had political functions, sometimes serving as stand-ins for absent officials or gathering intelligence when visiting other courts.[20]

The interesting thing about van Pelt's argument, however, is that these functions seem to have been present alongside strikingly scatological foolery. She refers to one of the most well-known Spanish fools of the Middle Ages, the French-born Antoni Tallander, nicknamed "Mosén Borra." Employed by Ferdinand I of Aragon in the early fifteenth century, Tallander is claimed to have been an educated writer and diplomat. However, in a frequently recounted anecdote he is said to have reacted with horror when the Grim Reaper appeared at a court pageant; and when Death tied him down and hoisted him up above the heads of the courtiers, the poor fool wet himself, causing urine to drip down onto the heads of the people below. Most historians, taking Tallander's other roles into consideration, deem this to have been a conscious performance of fear, realistic down to the very last drop.[21] Only Francesc Massip Bonet adds a cautious note, saying that the theatricals might have been convincing enough to frighten the fool, or that Tallander added some touches of his own when he reported the incident to the chronicler.[22] Intriguingly, even fools of the artificial type appear to have been mocked and manhandled from time to time, and this might reflect a more negative attitude towards artificial fools than toward natural fools.

Up until the time of the Renaissance, theologians and philosophers had trouble deciding whether "idiots" or "fools" should be considered human. To some, certain aspects of irrationality could be valued positively, as in the innocence of children, but since Aristotle, man had been conceived of as the "rational animal," and rationality was a sign that man had been created in the image of God. The absence of reason, then, would be a just cause for considering idiots as socially inferior or insensitive to hardship. But in discerning between various types of folly—between folly and idiocy, folly and stupidity, and so on—thinkers such as Thomas Aquinas concluded that in natural fools, who are fools by nature, folly is not a sin, because "no sin arises in us from nature," whereas people who act stupidly or who feign folly are sinful.[23] Correspondingly, medieval scholars such as Konrad of Megenberg and Gervase of Tilbury contended that natural fools should be considered divinely influenced marvels, things that come about "through the complete revocation of natural laws by direct divine interference."[24] This type of reasoning has sometimes been connected to the notion of "holy folly," but this concept originally derives from the religious idea that prophets or mystics who are uncorrupted by earthly desires will be viewed as fools by those around them. This concept was then reinterpreted as an encouragement to ascetics to feign foolish or irrational behaviour.[25] To the living conditions of men and women with what would today be classified as intellectual disability, such conceptions most likely had a very small significance.

When reviewing the learned debate on folly and idiocy in the centuries leading up to the sixteenth century, then, it is clear that although the attitude toward natural fools often appears sympathetic, it was conflicted and ambivalent, and the convoluted reasoning that one encounters in theological treatises seldom found its way into daily life. And although the harsh medieval attitude towards lunatics was on the wane, so was the protective spirit of medieval convents. We can study philosophical, theological, and medical writings on folly as long as we like, but we must accept that the general picture is unavoidably heterogeneous. The question is, How does it change when we consider the practice instead of the theory?

What principles guided the behaviour of people in the Renaissance court, and how did they apply to the fool? A royal court is of such a nature that role-playing becomes customary and sincerity rare. The theatricality of the Renaissance court is a theme picked up by many scholars studying the period. Not least Stephen Greenblatt, who goes so far as to assert that the very concept of theatricality itself "arose from conditions common to almost all Renaissance courts: a group of men and women alienated from the customary roles and revolving uneasily around a centre of power, a constant struggle for recognition and attention."[26] But does this theatre also include the court fool? Is he playing a role in the same way as the noble courtiers? Or was his place closer to that of kitchen helper or servant, individuals who were presumably not embraced by the mannered and theatrical performances of the people closest to the king?

T. J. Clark applies this question of sincerity and theatricality to the seventeenth-century portraits of court fools by Velazquez, asking, "What's more difficult: seeing through, or deep inside, the people who surround you, or seeing them in a way that stops at the facts of this or that expression—that doesn't imagine some secrecy informing them?" It is a question, Clark contends, that is especially pivotal in a court society, "in which keeping things superficial, and therefore not subject to malicious misinterpretation, may be a virtue, not to say a survival skill."[27] Clark says this in a discussion of Velazquez's court portraits, but he refrains from discussing some of his portraits where fools look out of the picture with an impenetrable gaze, incredulous or even defiant. These pictures show us fools and court dwarfs in poses and with facial expressions that defy characterisation. Some critics have asserted that Velazquez tacitly conveys his sympathy with their lot by depicting them in this way, but one might also apply the perspective that Clark implicates: that these fools express what Erving Goffman once referred to as "role distance," or what Clark calls "an achieved dis-illusion, a partial detachment from role; perhaps even the idea of living *with* illusion in full knowledge."[28]

The guiding principle of early modern courtiers was the dissimulation promulgated by the Italian courtier Baldassare Castiglione in his influential manual *The Book of the Courtier* (*Il Cortegiano*), first published in 1528. Dissimulation has been characterised as "a mode of speech replete with hidden meanings which allow one to speak one's truth."[29] In other words, self-control and letting one's thoughts and emotions go unexpressed unless tastefully disguised so as not to arouse too much unease. But Castiglione and those who were inspired by him never included the fool in this advice. When Cervantes tells of Don Quixote and Sancho Panza's visit to a ducal court, the former's unskilled attempt at dissimulation and the latter's complete inability to achieve dissimulation are comically underlined.[30] Fools were supposed to be natural and unaffected, displayed in their raucous practical joking and vulgar outspokenness. This is where the distinction between natural and artificial fools made occasionally in Renaissance writings emerges, but it rests on an ideal and perhaps even wishful thinking rather than on a portrayal of the reality. The mischievous nature of Cacurgus in *Misogonus*, mentioned in the previous chapter, illustrates the nobility's potential unease with not knowing for certain whether one's fool was a real natural or merely feigned idiocy. Clark's "detachment from role" and the sometimes ambiguous gaze of Velazquez's fools and dwarfs indicate an elusive self-consciousness—the freedom inside the fool's mind expressed in the inability of the people around him to know for certain about his mental state. We will have occasion to return to this ambivalence in our investigation of William Somer, for although his life and person are documented only in fragments, he crops up in many different places. Both the difficulty of determining what type of fool he was and the apparent indifference of his contemporaries concerning this tell us something of the role of the fool in the sixteenth century and of the Renaissance conception of comedy.

The question of role is fundamental in the consideration of the fool, for the definition of the Renaissance fool appears to be his exclusion from the ubiquitous role-playing going on at court. The point of the fool was that he didn't play a role. At the same time, the nature of role-playing or self-presentation, as theorised by sociologists, is that it encompasses everyone. Was the disabled natural labelled as a fool to such an extent that he began to "overact"? The concern of the naturalness of the fool reveals his function. He was supposed to be a reminder of the world outside, a small piece of the world of the commoners inside the palace walls, and as such a part of a world where affectation and role-playing in the minds of the nobles did not exist. But were the fools there simply to remind the courtiers and kings of this other world, working as a sort of memento mori, or were they there as an embodiment of the power exerted over this world by royalty and nobility? In her book on views of the intellectually disabled during the Middle Ages and the Renaissance, Irina Metzler refers to Yi-Fu Tuan's theory of domination and affection, in which he describes Renaissance fools as treated and viewed as human pets. Differences in physical appearance and intellectual capacities were "used as justification for domination and subservience." But the domination gave way to consideration. The precursor of modern charity is to be found, according to Metzler, in the compassion and affection of treating kept fools in the same way as pets.[31]

The appropriation of Tuan's notion is interesting, but I wonder if "human pet" is the best way to describe the domestic fool. Tuan's book is riddled with unfounded speculations and condescending attitudes toward what is sometimes described as the "backward" cultures of the past, which means that he sometimes reproduces the superior stance that he is bent on dissecting.[32] But what the thinking of Tuan and Metzler together with Clark and Goffman points to are a few intriguing suggestions that we might consider as we examine the case of Somer. These include the premise that the keeping of fools represented a search for authenticity. According to such an assumption, everyone is playing a role—only the fool is being himself. And the idea of the fool as a pet might point us in the direction of a more circumscribed definition of the fool as a sort of mascot or charm. In her influential book on the history of the fool, Enid Welsford considers the importance of ancient traditions in which fools in ritual practice are tokens of good luck, used to protect against the Evil Eye or bad luck. She notes rituals of the Graeco-Roman world, India, and medieval Europe in which the fool is detached from all the other participants because he is used to burden the misfortune of the others in the form of a scapegoat. The fool was seen as immune from the Evil Eye and could thus serve the purpose of a mascot, a role which she speculates might have lived on in the Renaissance court fool.[33]

Mascot, scapegoat, human pet, or exemption from the all-encompassing role-play of court society? Scholars have cast the fool in many roles over the years, but there are clear patterns when the conditions of foolery are in focus. My main purpose is to show the reality and practice of fools and fool culture as opposed to the ideology and philosophy of keeping fools, which has generally been the topic when scholars have dealt with the fool. Such research has produced and reproduced familiar notions concerning how the fool was free to speak his mind before the king, how the fool mirrored the vanities and stupidities of the king and his courtiers, how the fool was supposed to cure the king of occasional melancholia, and how he could be relied on to speak the truth, not being a calculating courtier with a hidden agenda. Almost all of these basic characteristics of the court jester can be found in scholarly works on the subject, but almost all of them are partly or wholly based on anecdotal and fictional evidence. I will show that this image of the functions of the fool is slightly touched up, and when we get closer to the reality, it more or less breaks down.

In her book on court jesters around the world, Beatrice Otto sternly defends the veracity of "the jester's function as adviser and critic," claiming that she has encountered only one writer who dismisses the truth-teller role of the fool as mere myth.[34] Thus she placidly ignores the decades of research pointing to the emergence of this myth in Erasmus, More, and Shakespeare.[35] One might counter by saying that it is difficult to find any documentation of a court fool being an honest adviser to a king that does not come from fiction or parables or touched-up hearsay. Many of these semifictional sources might contain much valuable information on real fools, such as the Italian *novelle* of Bandello or Sacchetti, advice literature by Castiglione and Erasmus, or stage comedies employing actual jesters as characters. But there seems to have been common tropes for how the fool was portrayed in literary form which cast him in a more symbolic form as truth teller and revealer of vanity and stupidity in the vein of ancient Roman slave clowns.

The insistence on the political or social importance of jesters as advisers and truth tellers seems to me more to be a sign of the historians' reluctance to consider the fool as "just" a fool. It is perhaps easier to justify writing about fools if they can be shown to have had an impact on government or political thinking. But such an argument does a disservice to the fool as a valuable object of study, since it tries to steer the topic into a sphere that it is not really about. By keeping the fools and their roles in focus, we tell a different but no less relevant story. It might be less about politics, power, or philosophy than some would like, but it is about inequality, norms, identity, and the fundamental discrepancy between how one conceives oneself and how others conceive you—a discrepancy that was possibly never greater than in the early modern court fools. By trying to imbue the fool with more "serious" subject matter than he was seen to represent at the time, and that he did not come into contact with himself, we paradoxically trivialise the ideas and roles that were closer and more pertinent to him.

In other words, it is high time we start taking the fool seriously.

CHAPTER 4

Origins

WILLIAM SOMER appears at the court of Henry VIII as if out of nowhere. He shares this fate with most other court fools of the Renaissance. In the next chapter, we will scrutinise the first occurrences of his name in court records, but before that, it is necessary to consider where he came from and to examine some of the claims concerning his origins. For a fool recruited from the lower orders of society, absence from records other than those of the court is hardly sensational. But can we be sure that his origins were not aristocratic?

There are two serious claims surrounding Somer's background. The problem with both is that they were made years after his death. Robert Armin, in his aforementioned account of Somer's activities, asserted that he was "borne in Shropshire, as some say."[1] This claim has the advantage of being the closest in time to Somer's own lifetime, but its wording does not inspire confidence, and there is little we can do with just the name of a county. The other claim is made by the eighteenth-century biographer James Granger in his *Biographical History of England* (1769), which says this about him:

> Will. Sommers was sometime a servant in the family of Richard Farmor, Esq. of Eston Neston, in Northamptonshire, ancestor of the earl of Pomfret. This gentleman was found guilty of a *præmunire* in the reign of Henry VIII. for sending eight-pence, and a couple of shirts, to a priest, convicted of denying the king's supremacy, who was then a prisoner in the goal [*sic*] at Buckingham. The rapacious monarch seized whatever he was possessed of, and reduced him to a state of miserable dependance. Will. Sommers, touched with compassion for his unhappy master, is said to have dropped some expressions in the king's last illness, which reached the conscience of that merciless prince, and to have caused the remains of his estate, which had been much dismembered, to be restored to him.[2]

This is all that Granger has to say about Somer, apart from a footnote, which reads: "That species of wit, which was the province of William Sommers, and other buffoons, in this, and several of the succeeding reigns, became the highest recommendation of a courtier, in the reign of Charles II."[3] This characterisation of Somer's wit and its influence on the conduct of courtiers does not quite bear scrutiny, as we will see, but the story of his original master and how he came to be a royal fool is specific enough to sound credible. Its main problem, pointed out by both Southworth and Mulryne, is that it is told more than two centuries after Somer's death. No historian has corroborated it, but neither does anyone appear to have tried.

The same story is told in greater detail in a chronicle from the Benedictine abbey of Teignmouth.[4] Here Richard Farmor is described as a "zealous Catholic" who earns his place in the annals as a hero of Catholic resistance by "not complying with the various changes in religion" during Henry's reign and assisting the Catholic priest Nicholas Thayne imprisoned at Buckingham. Farmor is said to have originally been a merchant at Calais who, having made a large fortune, settled in great comfort at the country house of Easton Neston, where he also employed a "jester," here referred to as "Will Somers." "This man," recounts the chronicle, "entertaining a grateful remembrance of his first master, and having admission to the king at all times, especially when sick and melancholy and near his end, let fall some lucky words which caused the king to give orders towards a restitution." The wording here is similar to Granger's, but it adds a detail that Granger conveniently omitted: "But," the chronicle says, "the king's death prevented [the restitution], and it was only in 1550 that his property was restored to him by the king's patents."[5] This cannot be the source of Granger's shorter version of the tale, however, as the chronicle appears to have been compiled in the mid-nineteenth century. The manuscript is now lost, since it was revised by the Teignmouth nuns in the early 1900s, but the part about Farmor is quoted at length as an aside in the published version of another abbey chronicle. The revised Teignmouth chronicle contains a note saying that the story about Somer and Farmor was taken from Hall's chronicle, but although the business of Farmor's punishment is mentioned by Hall, there is no mention in any edition of Hall's chronicle of Somer or his relationship with Farmor. The story, then, must derive from somewhere else, possibly an older abbey chronicle lost to us, a different Tudor chronicle, or simply folklore.[6]

Is there any other way of verifying this story? Thanks to the more extensive information on Richard Farmor given by the Benedictine chronicle, we can at least trace him to Henry VIII's time. Since the family name has subsequently been changed to Fermor, this is the name by which he is usually referred to. J. J. Scarisbrick has singled him out as "a remarkable (and neglected) man" of religious dissent who stands out as a rare "actively dissident" layman quite late in the century.[7] The affair of his downfall is well documented. On the basis of his alleged relationship with Thayne, he was charged with defying Henry's newly instated invalidation of papal authority. Fermor was committed to the Marshalsea Prison but was subsequently allowed to retire modestly to a village in Northamptonshire. His wealth was reinstated to him after Henry's demise, and in the last years of his life he acquired several new manors, making him a rich man at the time of his death in 1551.[8] No documents relating to this business make any mention of the potential influence of a fool, and perhaps they wouldn't, based on the general status of fools at this time and the seemingly unofficial nature of his influence. Fermor's name crops up frequently in the letters and papers of Henry's reign, first in his position as a powerful wool merchant, then as a merchant of the staple at Calais, and finally in relation to his recusancy. Richard's brother William also commonly appears in the records, and it seems that while Richard was punished for his disloyalty, William managed to stay in the clear, retaining his position as an attorney, high sheriff of Oxfordshire, and member of Parliament. Interestingly, William's main place of residence was Somerton Manor, which he had built himself close to the Oxfordshire village of the same name. The proximity of the names William and Somerton here risks sparking our imagination. There were other fools who are known to us only by the nicknames given to them by their employers, nicknames deriving from a trait or their place of origin.

Even though Granger's and the Benedictine chronicler's coupling of Fermor and Somer is made more than a century after their deaths, the considerable knowledge about Fermor displayed by both makes them quite trustworthy. Somer's service in the Fermor family does not contradict a possible background in Shropshire, although Armin is quite reticent about this information and does not say anything further, apart from pointing out in an anecdote involving Somer's uncle that he has travelled to court from Shropshire. A search through the relevant court records from the time of Somer's early service yields several intriguing albeit frustrating occurrences of the name Somer. A letter from courtier Sir William Kingston to Lord Lisle in September 1533, for instance, mentions a servant of Sir Edward Nevill called "Harry Somer, th[e] bearer, which the King is good lord unto," and who has "continued in the Court many years with Master Neville."[9] In the early 1530s, there are also several references in the court papers to a Thomas Somer, who was a successful stock-fishmonger and had several dealings with Thomas Cromwell.[10] Perhaps the most intriguing appearance of the name William Somer is in connection with the inheritance of the Hampshire woman Alice Lynne, or Lende, who died in 1524, leaving as heir her grandson William Somer, who by that time is said to be eight years old. The name and age are right, and in 1544 there is a warrant declaring that William Somer is now "of full age"; but upon further investigation we learn from an inquisition of 1553 that this Somer has died.[11] As we will see in the next chapter, the year of Mary's accession to the throne was one of Somer the fool's busiest periods at court.

Frustrating though the search for William Somer's background may be, it is not really in the actual specification of his place of birth or parentage that we learn about him, but in the office that he eventually held and the implications that this had. The absence of records or clear references to his origins strongly indicates what is implied throughout his career as a fool—namely, that he came from a humble background. Any nobleman showing signs of intellectual disability or eccentricity is unlikely to have been exhibited as a fool and would probably have been kept in the care of the family or with the help of a keeper, in as discreet a manner as possible.[12] We learn more about how Somer may have been recruited by looking at how other contemporary fools came to court. The recruitment of an artificial court fool would not have been particularly mysterious; it was probably similar to the recruitment of minstrels, tumblers, or other skilled entertainers. But how were natural fools engaged? There is one illuminating passage from a letter by Thomas Bedyll, one of the commissioners appointed by Thomas Cromwell to carry out visitations of monasteries and nunneries after the first Act of Supremacy had made the king head of the church. Bedyll writes from Spalding in Lincolnshire on 26 January 1536, having recently visited Crowland Abbey:

> Where I have written lately to you two or thre tymes of sad maters now I have occasion to write unto you of a cause of

myrthe ordeyned to temper sadnes. Ye know the Kings grace hath one old fole: Sexton as good as myght be which becaws of aige is not like to continew. I have espied one young fole at Croland which in myne opinion shal be muche mor pleasant than ever Sexton was in eny parte and he is not past XV yers old: which is every day newe to the hear. And albeit I meself have but smal delectacon in folys (I am made of so hevy a nator) yet emong a greate nu'br which I have herd spoken I have thought the same one of the best that I have herd and I beleve you wol so think when ye here hym. He wol be very m'ch cort and the King's grace shall have moche pleas'r by such parsetime shall make both us gentilmen & gentilwomen merry please you to send to thabbot of Croland for him and verily ye shall do the King's grace as grete pleas'r as may hav in any suche thing.[13]

The king's fool Sexton, to whom we shall return, was apparently getting on a bit, but all the same it is curious that the king should be on the lookout for a fool, since Somer had already come to court by this time. Whatever the case, the passage sheds some light on how natural fools could be recruited. The visitations made by Cromwell's commissioners around the time of Somer's first appearance in court records might have been a source for the "talent scouting" that appears to have gone on continuously. Although nothing seems to have come of the fool at Crowland—he is never mentioned in letters again—it is not impossible that this is how Somer came to court. There is a record in the State Papers of 1535 related to a visitation of a nunnery that contains reference to a petition from five young women—Jane Gowryng, Frances Somer, Mary Pilbeam, Barbara Larke, and

Bridget Stravye, "whose ages are respectively 23½, 22, 21, 20, and 15"—who wish to be "revested and come into their religion." The surname of one of them is intriguing, of course, and an addition to the entry provides further interesting dimensions: "Desire also to know whether Margaret Fitzgared, 12 years of age, being dumb and deaf, and Julian Heron, 13 years, an idiot fool, shall depart or no."[14] It was not uncommon for nunneries and monasteries to admit "idiots," a practice that was increasingly viewed with suspicion during the time of the dissolution, but was also in accordance with medieval theology.[15] The occurrence of the surname Somer and talk of a young "idiot fool" in the same entry are certainly suggestive but too vague to allow us to draw any conclusions. What this record can serve as, however, is an indication that people with learning disabilities who were in the care of abbeys around the country were encountered during the visitations and—as seen in Bedyll's letter—made contenders for the role of court fool.

The physical and personal distance between royal court and village life was short enough to allow men and women who distinguished themselves with an eccentric turn of mind or a disability that was considered amusing to be noticed by officials. Later anecdotes reinforce this image. It is said that Richard Tarlton, the Elizabethan clown, was in the field "keeping his Father's Swine" when a servant in the employ of the Earl of Leicester happened upon him and "was so pleased with his *happy unhappy* answers, that he brought him to Court, where he became the most famous Jester to Queen Elizabeth."[16] Similarly, the French king Henri III is claimed to have engaged the long-serving female fool Mathurine, who was originally working in the field canteen of the Picardian regiment, because he enjoyed her outspokenness and sharp tongue.[17] Although most evidence on such recruitments is anecdotal, we can be more certain that an alternative way of obtaining a fool was to get them from another household. We have already learned that Somer may have been transferred from the household of Richard Fermor to the royal household, and it is commonly believed that Henry VIII's former fool, Sexton, was also obtained in this way. The source for this story is George Cavendish's biography of Cardinal Wolsey, written between 1554 and 1558, and thanks to its proximity to Wolsey's own lifetime, as well as Cavendish's background as a servant in Wolsey's household, it is often taken to be as true an account of the events as possible. Here it is related that Wolsey, at the time of his fall from grace, gave his own fool to the king in order to appease him. When the king's man was to take away the fool to court, however, Cavendish describes how he fell into a rage and made such a struggle that it took six strong men to control him.[18]

This fool is never named, but John Southworth manages to tally the probable date of this event with the first appearances of the fool Sexton, also called "Patch," in the court accounts.[19] It is a scene that might shed some light on the possible procurement of Somer from the incriminated Fermor. It is probable that the king would be reluctant to appoint as his personal fool a completely untried new talent, preferring to secure someone who had proved his mettle with a previous master. If so, this might make up an illuminating backstory for a new relationship that by some indications got off to a bumpy start.

CHAPTER 5

Place

WHEN LOOKING for William Somer or any other court fool, it is logical to start with the records of the court. Following in the steps of previous historians who have managed to shed some light on him, I begin this search by considering what sort of picture we might gain from these records. Many have been studied before—most of them quite swiftly and out of context—while several other references have remained overlooked until now. By dwelling on these sources, we can consider Somer within the context of the court and acquire an impression of his place and status there. The earliest references indicate that he was definitely not the first of Henry VIII's fools. The king employed a number of fools in the first decades of his reign before the name of William Somer appears.[1] The fool whose name appears most often in the privy purse accounts of the 1520s is Sexton, who is commonly believed to be the fool known as Patch, which was probably his nickname. As touched on in the previous chapter, Patch was given to the king by Cardinal Wolsey, in whose household he was originally employed, and he is usually identified as a natural fool. John Heywood recorded one of his jests in a brief rhyme—when the cardinal implores Patch not to have a drink because he has a sore leg, the fool replies, "I drink on tother side."[2]

Before the full name of Somer starts to appear in the records, we find a few intriguing references to two men called "little guilliam" and "great guilliam," or sometimes "the two guilliams," beginning in December 1529. There are a couple of payments of "hose" for "the two Guilliams" together with lists of names that include Sexton, or Patch. In April 1530, they receive a payment "for their howsell."[3] In March 1531 we learn that Little Guilliam has been paid a small sum "for his dyet" and for "being sike at pety Johns," which might be a reference to an almshouse. Directly following this entry is a payment of twenty shillings on the same day "for a Rebecke for great guilliam."[4] A rebecke (or rebec), a three-stringed instrument played with a bow, was a precursor to the modern violin. The next month there is a payment to "a surgeon that heled litle guilliam," and then in August of the following year, thirty shillings was paid "to graunde guilliam by the kings comaundement for his surgery, when he was syke at London."[5] These two mysterious men were apparently court entertainers and recipients of charity at the same time; both were ailing and in frequent need of monetary aid. It is tempting to see in their names an indication of William Somer's first entry into royal patronage, perhaps as the son of Great Guilliam, but a reference to the minstrels Guilliam Dufayt and Guilliam de Trosshis in 1538, two instrumentalists presumably from the continent, rules out this possibility, and we are back to square one.[6]

When our man finally appears with his full name in the records, he is neither "Little William" nor "Guilliam" but "William Somer, our foole." The entry is dated 28 June 1535 and comprises a long list of new clothes entered into the royal wardrobe accounts:

> It'm for making of a dubblette of wursteede, lyned with canvas and cotton, alle of oure greate warderobe, for William Som'ar, oure foole. It'm for making of a coote and a cappe of grene clothe, fringed with red crule, and lyned with fryse, alle of oure greate warderobe, for our saide foole. It'm for making of a dublette of fustian, lyned with cotton and canvas, alle of oure greate warderobe, for oure same foole. It'm for making of a coote of grene clothe, with a hoode to the same, fringed with white crule lyned with fryse and bokerham, alle of oure greate warderobe, for oure foole aforesaid. It'm for making of a do coote with a hoode of grene clothe, fringed with crule of red and white colours, and lyned with bokerham, alle of oure greate warderobe, for oure said foole.[7]

The list is long: two doublets, one of fustian and one of worsted, both lined with canvas and cotton; two green coats, one fringed with white embroidery, the other with red; and a green cap. Are we to assume that this range of clothing is made for a newly appointed fool? The court accounts do not appear to contain any earlier explicit allusions to a fool of this name, but Somer is mentioned several times in John Heywood's interlude drama *Witty and Witless*, probably written somewhat earlier. The wording "our fool" likewise does not lead one to think of a completely new member of the household. John Southworth asserts that the long list of items is an indication that Somer is here being outfitted for the first time, and yet there are equally long lists of items for him in the wardrobe accounts from Mary I's reign. The accounts of September 1557, for instance, contain the following entry:

> ITEM to Richarde Tysdale Taylor for making of a Coate of grene clothe planne for the saide William Somer our foole lined with blacke Cotton for making of a Coate of grene clothe garded with grene veluett and lined with Cotton for making of a gowne and a Jerkin of blewe Damaske guarded with Carnation veluett the jerken lined with cotton for two dublettes of Canvas lined with canvas and Lockeram And a dublett of Blacke fustian lined with Canvas & Cotton all of our greate warderobe.[8]

An entry from March of the following year reads:

> ITEM to Rycharde Tysdale TAYLOR for makynge of a Coate for the saide Wiliam Somer of clothe garded with russett velluet and lyned with Cotton And for makynge of a wynter Gowne for him of clothe the sleves lyned with Cotton and for makynge of a Coate of playne clothe for hym lyned with Cotton for making of two Petycoats of flanen and for makynge of two doublettes for him of fustian lyned with Cotton all of oure greate Warderobe.[9]

Anyone who would like to make a study of Somer's clothes has a wealth of material to base their conclusions on, but this is too tempting a source for anyone who looks for material on court fools and is left frustrated. I will here limit myself to some aspects of Somer's wardrobe that might have a bearing on the bigger picture—for instance, the fact that so many of the items of clothing made for him were green, or the large quantities of buttons that were ordered for him (more on this below).

That court fools are most visible in the wardrobe accounts of early modern courts surely says something of their role being primarily visual and decorative. If we try to visualise the clothes, they might tell us something about how the conception of fools was translated into a visual style represented by the clothes—the greenness of Somer's dress might be an example of this—and in some instances the clothing of fools contained visual puns or joking allusions to their traits or disabilities. But the wealth of the wardrobe records also paradoxically reveals the lack of other records. What happened to the fools after they were kitted out? Some of them were immortalised in portraits (mainly painted ones), but there were also sculptures and statues, especially in Renaissance Italy.[10] We also know that they provided witty remarks at court and entertained at festivities or pageants. There are occasional records of wages or gifts. Somer's name can be found in scattered places in the records of the Tudor court, but its appearance is irregular and sometimes his absence is conspicuous. His name is not included in lists of payments made to musicians and minstrels, for instance, and it is clear that the work of fools, or of this fool, was something quite set apart from the conventional type of entertainment.[11] Was the fool's entertainment more interactive, more spur of the moment? We like to think so, perhaps, but we are also in some ways affected by modern depictions of medieval fools, not least Sir Walter Scott's formative portrayal of Wamba in *Ivanhoe*, whose every uttering is comically foolish in a way that never quite betrays whether he is unintelligent or acting the part. A similar depiction is the one of Patch in Hilary Mantel's *Wolf Hall*, where the fool is joking disarmingly in threatening situations as if he is always on the job.[12]

So where does Somer's name appear in the court records when he is not being given new clothes? A ferryman's bill among the state papers for January 1547 concerns the transporting of horses on the Thames on Christmas Eve. In all, fourteen horses were taken from Westminster to Hampton Court—three of which were the king's own horses, the rest belonging to various court officials, including a Mr. Awdley, a Mr. Jarnyngham, a man simply referred to as "Edmond," and "Wyllyam Sommers."[13] This record places Somer, unsurprisingly perhaps, among the retinue of people present at the king's Christmas celebrations. But does it mean that Somer lived permanently at Whitehall Palace or simply that he lived in London and was taken to Hampton Court only for the festivities? Several earlier histories state that Somer, along with Sybil Penn, Edward VI's nurse, was given a permanent apartment at Greenwich Palace during Edward's reign, but this assertion seems to hail from legend rather than records.[14] It is doubtful whether Somer or any other court fool lived in the royal palaces, and yet, he was regularly in attendance and periodically given so many clothes that he must at least have slept among the lowly servants every so often. Or perhaps, as Armin says, he slept among the spaniels?

Since we cannot be certain when Somer was appointed, it is unclear whether some of the remarks on court fools found in records of the 1530s refer to him or to some predecessor.

Records of the previous decades contain such names as "Marten the fool" and "Dick the fool," but after the 1520s only Sexton and Somer are mentioned. Thomas Cromwell's investigation into John Dryver, the prior of a convent in 1532, who was suspected of preaching against the king, contains an interesting passage. In a deposition given by one of the prior's associates, Dryver is claimed to have been telling tales of the king at the dinner table one night:

> Amongst the which one was that a certain fool, whose name this deponent knoweth not, named by the said Prior to be the King's fool or dysert,[15] which (as the said Prior alleged) was by divers of the King's servants so handled that he was compelled to fall from his horse back; which communication grew by way of exhortation, saying unto his convent there present, that they should keep good religion, saying that the fool should say at the time of his fall, and after that he was set upon his horse again, that the King should have a fall shortly.[16]

This would not be the last record of a rough handling of a fool. In July 1535, Eustace Chapuys, imperial ambassador to Charles V of Spain, appended a ciphered post scriptum in a letter to the Spanish statesman Antoine Perrenot de Granvelle. One of Granvelle's clerks had it deciphered, and it read: "Le roy d'Angleterre a cuyde tuer son fol, quest ung innocent, pour ce quil disoit et parloit bien de la Royne et Princesse et disoit Ribalde a la concubine et bastarde a sa fille et a este banny de court et la recelle le grand escuier." The English translation included in the *Calendar of State Papers* is the one commonly quoted: "He the other day nearly murdered his own fool, a simple and innocent man, because he happened to speak well in his presence of the Queen and Princess, and called the concubine 'ribaude' and her daughter 'bastard.' He has now been banished from Court, and has gone to the Grand Esquire, who has sheltered and hidden him."[17] Does this refer to Somer, or was it the exit of an earlier fool, who had already started to grow out of favour even before Somer was appointed? John Southworth believes that this recounts the last royal appearance of Sexton, who disappears from the records shortly after.[18] Alison Weir, on the other hand, assumes that the passage concerns Somer, and even claims that the grand esquire referred to by Chapuys, Nicholas Carew, had "dared" Somer to insult the queen and the princess, an interpretation that appears unfounded.[19] The last mention of a payment to Sexton in the privy purse accounts dates from 1532, and there is no record of him after that, whereas Somer, as seen, had by now been appointed.

Even though it gives a tidier picture to think that Chapuys here reports on the dismissal of Sexton, it might be more reasonable to assume that the fool was Somer. If taken together with the above story of the manhandling of the fool on the horse, it implies a rough start to Somer's career as court fool. The well-documented unpredictable nature of the king certainly makes it feasible that Somer would be a victim of his bouts of rage, and then taken into favour once more when it had all blown over. There are a few mentions of "Anthony, the fool" in wardrobe accounts of late 1539, which implies the engagement of a new fool for the court.[20] In the 1540s, the name of Jane Foole, who was the fool of Catherine Parr, starts to appear, as well as a reference to "Thomas Browne, the Queen's fool," on 21 April 1546.[21] This should not lead us to think that Somer was dismissed by Henry and then reinstated by Edward, since he is present alongside Jane Foole in the 1545 portrait of the family of Henry VIII, and several contemporary allusions to him in letters also place him at the court in the 1540s. We should probably not read too much into this infrequent nature of a fool's occurrence in court records, but it does raise questions concerning the fool's place in the royal household. To what extent was the fool a servant like any other, or should we instead place him among the courtiers and nobility?

The English court during the age of the Tudors was chiefly divided into two main sections: the chamber and the household. The role of the chamber was political, and its core was the privy chamber, comprising the men closest to the monarch: noble-born gentlemen who would wait on and attend the king. Henry VII established the privy chamber, but it evolved during the reign of his son into an essential group of friends who accompanied him in his daily activities and influenced his decisions. The great chamber, the other section of the chamber, was headed by the lord chamberlain, who supervised the public rooms of the court where the king received official visits and all other public arrangements were handled. The great chamber included positions such as physicians, tutors, chaplains, scholars, artists, and young courtiers in training. The purpose of the household, on the other hand, was to provide the king with the basic essentials—food, lodging, cleaning, transport, and so on. This was the section of the court where menial servants were employed and the possibility of political influence was virtually nonexistent. The departments of the household included the kitchen, the larder, the pastry, the scullery, the laundry, the pantry, and the bakehouse. Porters, maintenance men, and musicians were likewise part of the household, and it also included the great hall, which served simpler food to the ordinary servants.[22]

Perhaps the most difficult person to place within the various departments and sections of the court is the court fool. The entertainment sectors comprised musicians, who, as we see, were a part of the household. However, the lord chamberlain was in charge of the "Revels Office" and its supervisor, the master of the revels, who oversaw the royal festivities and performances of plays and masques. But a closer look at accounts and lists of names from these sectors during the sixteenth century does not suggest that the fools belonged strictly to either. Somer's name appears in records related to the master of the revels, but only very rarely, indicating that his presence was in the form of guest appearances. As we have seen, he is not included in the lists of musicians and minstrels. Several departments and appointments of the court operated independently, being part of neither the chamber nor the household, such as the master of the horse, who supervised the royal stables and the men who took care of everything surrounding the royal hunting, a vast operation. The Master of the Revels and the Great Wardrobe—two departments where fools' names occasionally appear—also had their own accounts. In short, the court was an unwieldy, and to a great extent disorganised, structure, and several royal officials, most notably Cardinal Wolsey and Thomas Cromwell, took it upon themselves to try to establish order, without really eliminating the partial disorder.

Although probably predating Somer's time at court, the Eltham Ordinances of 1526 provide much comprehensive insight into the structure and personnel of the Tudor court. The ordinances, laid out as a proposed reform of the court by Cardinal Wolsey in order to regulate its organisation and expenditure, were a measure to limit the expenses of the court after the costly wars with France in the previous decade. The document lays down strict rules for every member of the royal household, including instructions for the serjeant of the bakehouse to ensure that a substantial amount of wheat is bought at the best price, instructions for the master cooks to give daily attendance to the king and his household and to make sure "their meates be good and sweete," detailed lists of exactly what provisions of food are to be given to each member of the household, and lists of which courtiers are to be given room in the stables for their horses. This last list is helpful in indicating who regularly resided at court, as it also details "th'appointment of herbigage [accommodation] to be ordinarie for all noble estates and others." The first titles in the list are unsurprising, containing officeholders such as a cardinal, a duke, a baron, a viscount, a marquis, and an earl; the knights of the king's council; six gentlemen of the privy chamber; and surgeons, physicians, grooms, and pages. The less illustrious but essential members of the household come next, including messengers, falconers, secretaries, maids, the cofferer, the treasurer, the lord steward, gentlemen ushers, and waiters. There are even entries for trumpeters and minstrels. Other expected members are left out, however. There are no cooks or kitchen staff, for instance. And no fool. In fact, the only reference to "the king's foole" in the entire Eltham Ordinances is in a subsequent list of horses to be kept for various court officials. This list details such positions as the groom of the stool, the clerk of the avery, the clerk of the stable, and the yeoman sadler, as well as several named individuals with no given titles. The fool is listed among a number of men associated with the stables, such as "besage men" (men in charge of saddle bags), "sumpter men," "the peckman," and "riders."[23] Several years later, in the inventory made of Henry VIII's possessions on the year of his death, a horse for the king's fool is mentioned yet again, but once more being the only reference to the presence of a fool at court.[24] It is curious to see that one of the rare recurring instances when the fool is mentioned in court records is in connection with his horse, and the fact that the court accepted responsibility for moving him suggests, if nothing else, that he was a regular attender.

The mobility of the fool appears to have been more important than any lodgings for him then. The date of the Eltham Ordinances might suggest that at that point the king did not have as well-liked and favoured a fool as Somer would become, at least judging from his posthumous reputation. The report of the royal commission of 1552 that was meant to scrutinise and restructure the court finances contains an extensive list of all the individuals employed by the court and given pensions and remunerations of numerous sorts. There are minstrels, musicians, players, and singers, but not a single fool is mentioned. The absence is striking, and one might be led to believe that the document was compiled at an interval of time when no fool was in court employ.[25] It requires some digging in the archives to find him. As we saw in the beginning of this

chapter, there were records of payments to fools and entertainers in the privy purse accounts of the 1520s. After 1532,
however, the records of these expenses are much less comprehensive. One of the few remaining insights into the privy
chamber finances is through the rare survival of a twenty-four-
foot roll of vellum containing an audit of the receipt and expenditure of Anthony Denny, the groom of the stool, from 1542 to
1548.[26] One of the main duties of the groom of the stool was
the keeping of the money reserved for the king's private use,
and this document thus contains several entries for all sorts of
expenses, from furniture and tools to labourers and apothecar-
ies. At the end of a long list of seemingly unrelated expenses
come the words "and also for the apparrell of Willm Somer and
sondrie boyes of the stable."[27] So he is still there, even though
he is once more mentioned only in relation to his clothes. And
a document of wardrobe accounts covering the end of 1552 and
early 1553 shows that he was indeed at court at the time of the
royal commission, since we find there an entry for the "making
of two new Gownes for Willm Sumer foole."[28]

What are we to make of this longtime recurrence of Somer's
name and the accompanying absence of it in certain records?
The picture it paints is of a court employee who is present at
the very heart of it—both spatially and functionally—while
at the same time being of such a lowly status as to be offered
little or no boarding. There are, to my knowledge, no records
of any court fool living within the precincts of the royal palaces during the Tudor age. The general impression one gets
from records of Somer's later years, after the death of Henry,
is of a man who is taken to court to appear on certain special
occasions, for old time's sake. The main administrative docu-

ments shedding light on Somer's role at court in his later years are the Revels accounts under Edward VI and a couple of detailed receipts.

The documents of the master of the revels at the time, Thomas Cawarden, contain numerous letters and receipts providing insight into the elaborate festivities arranged around Christmastime. The Revels Office operated directly under the privy council, and during the reign of the boy king, the spectacles were particularly extravagant, perhaps as a way of entertaining the young monarch. For the various players and performers involved in the games and frolics, all sorts of colourful costumes were made, together with props ranging from pasteboard crowns and wigs to fake swords and ceremonial staffs. Many of the things made for the festivities were toy weapons and armour, such as maces and visors. A common ingredient in these shenanigans was the mock combat, a form of entertainment that involved court fools and dwarfs in many European countries.[29] The extremely sumptuous Revels of Christmas 1552–1553, which were headlined by the poet and member of Parliament George Ferrers, included a large retinue of jugglers, tumblers, fools, and friars who would challenge each other to combat on hobbyhorses.[30] William Somer was not present at this particular event, it seems, but on the two preceding Christmases we find his name in the accounts: first in a payment for the painting of his garments (an entry made in a list of payments for visors, swords, and maces but without any explicit indication that these were for Somer), and then in two, more revealing, entries the following year.[31] The first was payment for a "triminge and overgyldinge of a Mace for william Soomer to atten the lorde of Mysrule," then payment for "one copper cheyne dubble gylded for ye lorde of mysrule & another for William Somer," and finally, a few entries down, "a devise by the kinge for a combat to be foughte with Wylliam Somer." This entry contains such items as "maske heddes" and "a harniss of paper boordes." For "the Lorde of mysrules foole" there was also an order for "one vyces dagger" and a "ladle with a bable pendante."[32]

The combative nature of the Christmas festivities was essential and related to most other forms of early modern carnival. The entries in the Revels accounts attest to this. For instance, apart from the fake weaponry, there is mention in the payments of coats of canvas being painted to look like chainmail. Ferrers is credited with arranging particularly overblown spectacles during his reign as Lord of Misrule, and the Edwardian festivities are seen as a brief zenith of Tudor Christmas festivals, although to some extent this must also depend on the scarcity of preserved records for previous festivals.[33] In Tudor festivals, the Lord of Misrule became a separate figure from that of the Vice, the precursor to the clown character of Elizabethan theatre, who appears in both medieval morality plays and seasonal festivals. The Lord of Misrule was the main figure of the ceremonies, and the Vice was his servant or minion. David Wiles points out that Lords of Misrule were generally recruited from amateurs, while the person who played the part of the Vice was a professional, returning in the role from year to year.[34] The Revels accounts give only one indication that William Somer was the Vice in these goings-on—the reference to the "vyces dagger" made for the "Lorde of mysrules foole"—but it is manifest enough. Somer was the Vice in at least one Christmas festival at court.

The question is what we should attach the greatest importance to: the fact that he took part in these festivities as the Vice or the fact that there are no records of him doing this in any other year. John Southworth diminishes somewhat the importance of this record by emphasising its isolated nature and speculating that such festivities are "not a world in which an innocent is likely to have been comfortable."[35] This might well have been the case, but the fact that he did play the part of the Vice also says something about his status and function. Most likely, the court desperately tried to find a place for the old fool under the reign of a child who was not able to appreciate the by-all-accounts more subtle and verbal nature of his usual conduct. As we will see in chapter 8, the gist of Somer's comedy and the things about him that the people around him treasured were not things likely to have been appreciated by a young boy. Then again, there are other indications that Somer's role was not wholly verbal but also symbolic or visual. This likely would have meant that he could be used for various purposes, and if Ferrers or Edward wanted him for the Vice, then he would have to comply.

The most striking aspect of Somer's appearance in the Revels accounts is of course the allusion to the combat in which Somer would take part. From the wording, it is not clear whether Edward would be the antagonist in this combat or whether he simply came up with the "device" for it. Curiously, however, it is not specified that the combat will be fought with the Lord of Misrule. Only Somer's and Edward's names are included. It is not improbable that it was another attempt to use the fool in a way more adapted to the comic taste of a boy. Either Somer engaged in this mock combat with the young king, or his opponent was Ferrers or any of the other fools or tumblers taking part in the performance, but the closeness of the names in this entry is surely indicative. I think the king took part and that many of the arrangements were designed to be enjoyed by a child whose heavy burden needed to be eased for Christmas.[36] Perhaps Somer was not so uncomfortable with this, or perhaps this type of game was even one of the rare things he did enjoy, but the king had simply grown out of this type of play by the following Christmas. In either case, this shows how Somer was not exempt from the types of uses fools and dwarfs were put to in courts all over Europe. Furthermore, this record is important as it contains the only mention of an archetypal fool's attribute—the ladle with a bauble—in conjunction with Somer's name. In no other written or visual records, as we will see, is Somer associated with typical fool props, which are really mainly seen in stereotypical images of fools rather than portraits of real fools. Within the context of festivals, however, fools and Lords of Misrule appeared as representatives of such stereotypes. They were the equivalent of the king's crown and sceptre, worn only on ceremonial occasions. Whether Somer used these attributes at other events, or earlier than this, is uncertain. Possibly this festival was an attempt to appropriate these and turn the former fool of the king's chamber into a more public ceremonial figure. The more extravagant clothes made for him during Mary's reign might support this interpretation.

This brings us to the receipts I mentioned earlier. These are two small scraps of paper found in a large box together with other miscellaneous documents of lesser importance from

the State Papers. Most of the papers in the box are of a finan-
cial nature: receipts for repair work and deliveries of goods,
as well as wages to various minor officials. The two papers
related to Somer are dated 1547 and occasioned by Edward's
coronation. The first begins "It[e]m to the laender for wassh-
ing of willm sommers .v. dussyn of shertes"[37] and then follows a list of items purchased for him, including two pairs of
gloves and a purse. Among these items, however, we also find
the entry: "Itm for shaving of willm—xij[d]." The second para-
graph begins "to the hooseare agea[n]st the cronac[i]on"—
the secretary is getting sloppy now—and lists three pairs of
hose of different colours, two pairs of stockings, and, to the
shoemaker, payment for four pairs of double-soled shoes and
two pairs of single-soled shoes. The second sheet of paper is
in a different hand but probably dates to about the same time,
although this must refer to a separate instance. Beginning
"For Wyllm Sumar," it enumerates, apart from a number of
items of clothing (such as six pairs of socks and a pair of
spurs), payment for two other services: at the top of the list is
"for shavynge of hym and poolynge," and at the bottom of the
list is "for wassheynge of hes fete."[38]

The clothes referred to in these receipts are interesting in
themselves, but it is the other items that I want to dwell on.
The first sheet says nothing about washing Somer himself,
only his clothes, but if the second sheet hails from the same
occurrence, then it is strange that there is another payment for
shaving him. It is likely that the washing was left out from the
first one, for whatever reason. In any case, it is curious that the
washing and grooming of the fool should be itemised in this
distinctive way, unless he has been absent from court for some

time and taken back for the pleasure of the new king. The conscious efforts to underpin Edward's legitimacy would surely have included reinstating his father's well-known fool. Anything that could strengthen the ties to the past was useful. And although there are no sources, it is not unlikely that Somer would have briefly left court after the death of Henry. The entries in these receipts can easily spur the imagination. Was he in a dishevelled state when taken back to court, and forced to be washed and bathed, with particular attention being paid to his feet? Had he gone about barefooted, soiling his feet to an unmanageable degree, or was he simply incapable of washing his own feet? The repeated references to shaving are also more revealing than one might think. As we shall see when reviewing his portraits, Somer's hair was always cropped when he appeared as court fool, but he also never appears with a beard of any sort. Beards were an important signal of masculinity in the Tudor period, but their symbolism was intricate. Even though 90 percent of Tudor male portraits show bearded men, as observed by Will Fisher, there were conditions that might excuse beardless men, such as religious convictions, youth, or occupation, as noted by Eleanor Rycroft.[39] When it came to fools, however, their childlike status made them an exception, which we will return to in the next chapter. Suffice it to say here that the shaving in these receipts points to the fact that Somer was once more taken up as court fool upon the ascension of Edward, and consequently he needed to be shaved to show who he was.

There is one last reference to William Somer in administrative court records that I would like to conclude with. In the wardrobe accounts of Mary's reign, there are, as mentioned, several extensive orders of clothes for the fool. There are notices of both items of clothing purchased and material ordered for the making of clothes. The entries mostly consist of so-and-so many lengths of silk fabric and various types of hoses, but one recurring category of objects in these entries becomes eye-catching the more you read. It is nothing special in itself, but it becomes so thanks to its volume.

I am referring to buttons. Other people mentioned in the accounts receive large quantities of buttons, but these are all manufacturers of clothes of some description. William Somer is given enormous quantities of buttons. In October 1554, he receives "thre dossen of grene buttons," then the following April "thirteen dosen and a haulf of round silke buttons of sundrie collours" as well as "two dossen buttons of grene silke and silver."[40] In April 1557, he is given "tenne dossen of silke buttons of diverse collors," and in September of the same year, "nyne dossen of buttons of diverse collours." In March of the following year he receives "two dosen of buttons with brode knottes," and in October "one grosse of Buttons with stalkes."[41]

Why so many buttons? Well, before we draw any foregone conclusions we should consider the rather large number of buttons required for some Tudor garments. One of the 1554 entries includes a further mention of "two dossen white buttons" said to be for a certain doublet. But this still seems like a lot of buttons, and one is tempted to think that Somer's clothes required more buttons than others'. An entry mentioning "eighte dosen of rounde sylke poyntes"[42]—the bands used to tie together items of clothing in the Renaissance—might be cited in this context as another example of the ubiquity in this age of devices for fastening and closing items of dress, but buttons might have been more important as simultaneously functional and decorative.[43] Their decorative use was facilitated by their relative lack of cost as compared with jewellery, but purely decorative buttons were uncommon, and when we look at the portraits of Somer in the next chapter, we shall see that the clothes he is wearing are not of the type requiring long lines of buttons. Neither did he wear the type of long protective coats sometimes associated with the intellectually disabled that were designed to keep them warm and shield them from harm.[44] Some of the later accounts hint that the clothes made for him were quite warm, perhaps owing to an increasing coldness or the draughty atmosphere of the palaces. To some extent, this might explain why his clothes needed to be closed up with many buttons, but it hardly explains in itself the enormous amounts ordered for him.

This is a mystery that brings us into the realm of his personal qualities rather than any general picture of contemporary clothing. Might one ascribe it to a tendency to lose buttons or to pull them off in bouts of rage, like some of the other fools described by Robert Armin? This is not implausible, although we lack sufficient supporting evidence to suggest that Somer was prone to such regular outbursts. Even if he was, it seems far-fetched to think that the buttons ordered for him would be both a direct consequence of this and the only testimony of it. It does, however, strike one as something vaguely indicative of his personality. Was he a collector of buttons? Did he do something with them outside of wearing them on his clothes? Did he sell them outside of court? The fool Simplicity in Robert Wilson's 1590 comedy *The Three Lords and Three Ladies of London* takes to selling buttons from a stall.[45] Having considered all the different references to William Somer in court records, perhaps it is here that we catch a glimpse of the person behind the name and the occupation—a hint of an inclination or an interest, an obsession even. But what this chiefly demonstrates is the frustration inherent in trying to tease out information about Somer and his role through these types of administrative records. We need other sources to learn more about him. Although these will never be as concrete as the entries in account books, they will allow us to see what can here be only indirectly gleaned—the doings and character of the fool.

CHAPTER 6

Features

THERE ARE traces of Somer in the court accounts, and there are references to Somer's character and wit in the writings of his contemporaries, but in between sit the portraits. Neither the impersonal data of the account record nor the interactive and emotional depiction of the letter writer, the painted portrait says everything and nothing. With the sometimes realistic and detailed portrayals by Renaissance painters, we now and then seem to come close to the faces of the individuals of this age, but at the same time the corresponding lack of further records, or the often enigmatic symbolism of Renaissance art, leaves the viewer frustrated. Renaissance fool portraits especially have the ability to entice with their rare documentations of plebeians, but when one endeavours to find out more about the fool in the painting, one almost always arrives at a dead end. The mythologisation and the indifference of the written record mean that we receive a tantalising impression of coming close to a person but are then never given the satisfaction of learning anything substantial about him.

Since the number of portraits of William Somer is so large—larger even than for many of the period's most illustrious noblemen and noblewomen—it seems appropriate to continue our advance towards the figure of Somer there. Having seen him in the accounts and delineated his approximate place at court, we now focus on him as a person and how he was perceived. The number of portraits of Somer is indicative, then, of the physical symbolism of fools, since many others were also documented in portraits, while the written record is tellingly scarce. But it also provides us with a first entry point into the matter of Somer's quality as a fool and the significance of his body and appearance in his role as court fool. At least three, possibly four, of the extant portraits of Somer were painted during his lifetime, even though two of the ones including Henry were done after the king's death. There is also one well-known engraving published in the early seventeenth century which demands our attention.

We begin with the perhaps most sumptuous painting in which Somer is portrayed: *The Family of Henry VIII.* Dated to around 1545, this picture, on an oblong canvas by an unknown artist of the Holbein school, depicts Henry on a canopied throne surrounded by his family: third wife Jane Seymour and Prince Edward, later Edward VI. A bit farther from this central group are, on each side, the princesses Mary and Elizabeth, both eventually queens. The room that the royals are standing in has two archways, one on each side. They open up to an outside garden, and in each opening we see the two court fools—one male, one female. On the left is a woman believed to be Jane Foole, and on the right we have Somer. Somer is standing in a curious pose, turning to the

FIGURE 2. *The Family of Henry VIII*, by an unknown artist, c. 1545. The Royal Collection; on display at Hampton Court Palace. Top: detail. Wikimedia Commons.

side with a slightly tilted head while a pet monkey sits on his shoulder with its hands on his scalp (fig. 2). Some commentators reckon that the monkey is checking his hair for lice,[1] but the animal is looking forward, not down, and its fingers are spread out rather than bent. Somer looks young, not older than thirty, but the picture is decidedly deceptive. Jane Seymour had been dead for eight years when the painting was presumably made. The age of Edward, born the same year as his mother Jane died, precludes the possibility that it would have been made much earlier than 1545, however.

If Somer came to court as a young man, the age of around thirty sounds reasonable, and the appearance of his rough-hewn features as depicted here can be compared to their more aged quality in later pictures. The most striking physical aspects are his protruding brow and hollow eyes, but there is no sign of the hunchback that he receives in some accounts.[2] His and Jane's placement in the garden setting is decidedly separate from the royal family, but their inclusion is interesting and unusual in a group portrait of this kind. A comparative picture is Rowland Lockey's group portrait of Thomas More and his family and descendants, in which More's fool Henry Patenson is seen looking in through a gap in the background arras.[3] Family portraits including fools abound in the seventeenth century, but in Tudor England they are still quite rare. The addition of the monkey is surely meant to suggest some sort of affinity, thus implicitly labelling Somer as a fool. This might be compared with the corresponding solitude of Jane Foole, whose folly is instead conveyed in her vacant facial expression and upturned head, as if she is looking towards the sky, unsuccessfully searching for a god. The monkey's placement, echoing the turned head of Somer, could almost be interpreted as symbolising the contents of Somer's head. There are occasional allusions to monkeys in the letters and papers of Henry VIII, including a letter mentioning Anne Boleyn's dislike of "such beasts" and notices of monkeys given as gifts, at one point to Thomas Cromwell.[4] Pet monkeys were evidently a natural presence at court, along with numerous other animals, both domestic and exotic, and they were not unusual in portraits of fools. A buffoon is seen playing with a monkey in the fresco at Castello del Buonconsiglio in Trento in 1531. More famously, the Spanish court dwarf Magdalena Ruiz would later in the century be portrayed together with her mistress, the Infanta Isabel Clara Eugenia, holding two monkeys in her arms.[5]

Somer's pose in this painting is also striking. He appears to be bowing in greeting to an unseen person who is standing next to him, out of view. Somer is turned in the king's direction, but since he is standing outside of the room, he cannot be bowing to him, even though this would seem to be the likeliest interpretation. In any case, the pose is an expression of submission and courtesy and sets him apart from the pose of Jane Foole, who seems to be elsewhere in her mind, hardly conscious of her immediate surroundings. Are we to take from this that Somer was less intellectually disabled than her, if at all?[6]

While Somer in this painting is distant from the king, even though his presence in such an important dynastic portrait is remarkable, he appears in another depiction some years earlier, alone with the king. This is in one of the illuminations of the psalter commissioned by Henry in 1540 from the French scribe Jean Mallard. In several of the illuminations,

Mallard depicts Henry as King David, who was believed to have written the psalms, and annotations by Henry's hand in the extant copy confirm that Henry appreciated this analogy.[7] One of the most explicit portrayals of Henry as David accompanies Psalm 53, which contains the line "The fool hath said in his heart, There is no God." Here Henry is seen sitting in a chamber playing the harp—used by King David to ward off evil spirits—while Will Somer is standing next to him, his back turned to the king (fig. 3). The image is unassuming and placid, but the arrogant pose of the fool is provocative and would probably have raised an eyebrow, if not more, if it had happened in real life. One would hardly expect a picture of Henry and his fool in cheerful camaraderie, enjoying a good joke together, but this composition is mysterious. Clearly it is meant to convey the ungodliness of the fool in some way. Somer's countenance is hard-set and almost sad as he clasps his hands in what seems to be fruitless prayer. At the same time the king looks towards the reader with a condescending expression, his lips shut tight as if trying to wish away the fool, or at least pretend he is not there. In fact, the overall impression is that both men are trying to ignore the other, as if the king is a bit uncomfortable at suddenly finding himself in the same image as his fool, and the fool does not quite know what to do in this unexpectedly respectable setting.

When we finally see Henry VIII and his famous fool in the same portrait, then, it is not an image of intimacy or warm feelings of any kind. Somer is not even treated as were later court dwarfs in portraits, with a kind of patronising care that contains at least some sort of emotion. It is tempting to view this double portrait as an indicator of Somer's importance at

FIGURE 3. Illumination from Henry VIII's psalter by Jean Mallard, 1540–1541. British Library.

court and to the king, but as the king's fool he would have been the most likely candidate for illustrating this psalm. Perhaps there is little more to it than that—a fool needed to be depicted, and Mallard went for the obvious choice. Somer's and Henry's lack of interaction should probably be read in conjunction with the text of the psalm, but apart from that, Mallard merely seems to have painted a portrait of Somer, appropriately with his hands in prayer. As a portrait, it is, in spite of its small size, one of the liveliest and most

realistic. Unlike the quite blank depiction of Somer's face in
the family portrait, he is here portrayed with sad eyes and
a worried mouth. We recognise the short hair and brow
ridge from the other picture, but here a stubble beard adds a
sense of this man's nature and living conditions. It is the pen-
sive, slightly turned gaze that makes the portrait come alive,
however. It whispers to us that this fool might be a bit hurt
by the unkind attitude of the psalm and the king.

Somer next appears in two group portraits depicting members of the royal family. A large portrait hanging at Boughton
House in Northamptonshire is believed to be a seventeenth-
century copy of a lost original. The original is presumed to
have been painted during Edward VI's reign, since he is the
central figure. He is surrounded on one side by Henry VIII
and Somer and on the other by the princesses Mary and Elizabeth. The extant painting is crudely done, but interesting to
us in that it shows Somer some years older than in the previous pictures, but not yet with the signs of age apparent in the
last portrait of him. The depiction of Edward is based on the
royal portraits of him painted by William Scrots around
1550–1552, which possibly serves to date this group portrait.[8]
Somer is here once more unshaved, and his protruding brow
and deep-set eyes are apparent. He casts a sideways glance
and purses his lips, looking a bit more devious than in other
depictions (fig. 4). The placement of him behind Henry is
telling, as this associates him with the reign of the old king
and presumably is what qualifies him for inclusion in this
painting. His looming, shadowy presence makes him quite a
mysterious figure, however. There is nothing to identify him
as a fool. By this time it appears to have become customary

FIGURE 4. *Portrait of Henry VIII and His Family,* by an unknown artist, seventeenth-century copy of lost original, c. 1550–1552. The Buccleuch Collections.

to portray Somer in a simple and unadorned fashion, a bit like a friar. Apart from the monkey in the 1545 painting, no attributes connect him with the business of foolery.

The late date of this recently discovered painting makes it difficult to draw any conclusions from it, but it might be compared with another group portrait which is dated to the reign of Queen Mary. Here Somer suddenly carries both a staff in his right hand and a small lap dog under his left arm. The dog has bells on its collar—the first explicit allusion to the conventional attributes of the court fool. Somer is here portrayed with more attention to detail and more artistic skill, but the vaguely mischievous expression of the previous painting is here exchanged for an ambivalent and slightly cagey visage (fig. 5). Of all the portraits of Somer, this is perhaps the most mysterious, not least because of the

FIGURE 5. Detail of *Posthumous Portrait of Henry VIII with Queen Mary and Will Somers the Jester*, by an unknown artist, 1550s. The Museum of Fine Arts, Houston.

relatively high level of realism and detail in the representation of his facial features. His protruding brow and cheeks can be seen in full view, creating an almost masklike face of furrows and blotches. But it is the penetrating gaze and faint, knowing smile that are the most striking. This is a far cry from the submissive and recoiling figure of the psalter and monkey portraits. The worried gaze of those earlier portraits is substituted with a calm and composed presence. One might be excused for doubting whether it is the same man as in the early portraits, but the recurring physical features and the incessant greenness of his clothes speak for themselves.

This painting probably hails from Mary's reign, judging from the absence of her Protestant siblings and the apparent purpose here of accentuating her closeness to her father king. But what is the fool doing here? Fool portraits generally during the early modern period are more common on the continent. Alongside the late seventeenth-century dwarf Jeffrey Hudson, Somer is probably the most depicted English court fool; and apart from Jane Foole, no other Tudor court fool is portrayed. Archie Armstrong, court jester to James VI, was depicted only in contemporary prints, and no painting of him seems to survive. The convention also generally seems to be to depict fools in solo portraits. During the seventeenth century especially, court dwarfs can be seen in the backgrounds of royal scenes in Spain, Italy, and England.[9] The function and symbolism of court dwarfs were of such a nature that they needed to be depicted together with the monarchs.[10] But portraits of kings or queens next to their fools are extremely rare. There is consequently no point of comparison in a Tudor context apart from the aforementioned family portrait of Thomas More.

The primary conclusion to be drawn from the portraits of William Somer is undoubtedly how popular or renowned he must have been, at least at the Tudor court. In the last two paintings we have considered, he seems to function as a symbol of continuity, a fixture of the court that ensures it is the same as it was in the reign of Henry when his heirs take over, one by one. This reading is supported by Somer's appearance in an Elizabethan dynastic allegory of the Tudor succession, in which Henry sits on the throne while blessing the reformation of Elizabeth as Mary and her Spanish husband are seen defeated after the Armada. This is an adaptation of a 1572 original, made around 1590. Somer is not included in the original, but the new version shows an oval on the far left edge of the picture with a portrait that can only be identified as Somer (fig. 6). Clearly the whole purpose of the image, to show and underpin the authority of Elizabeth, was seen as being helped by the inclusion of the old fool. It is as if including him in circumstances with a dynastic purpose was considered natural. As "the king's fool," Somer is usually associated solely with Henry or the following monarchs, but he could also be considered an entertainer in the close circle of the royal family. Perhaps the importance of his horse is a sign that he not only moved along with the court but also moved between the king and his children.

Somer's inclusion as a convention, however, puts him in a role that is somewhat different from the common notion of the court fool as a mere entertainer. The family portraits of Edward's and Mary's reigns indicate this, but the 1590 allegory underpins the impression that Somer was turning into a good luck charm for the Tudor dynasty. To have him in the background of a dynastic portrait would ensure the success of the next generation. In a tradition that probably begins with the 1545 family portrait, and is then taken up by each of his children on their accession, Somer is invoked not as a fellow of mirth or jesting, as are later fools like Armstrong or Tom Derry, but as a looming, slightly uncanny figure, included more for his symbolic role and long time in service than for any other reason. The tradition might have originated as a mere fluke that by the time of Elizabeth's allegory had become common practice. His continuous presence in

FIGURE 6. *An Allegory of the Tudor Succession: The Family of Henry VIII*, by an unknown artist, c. 1590. Top: detail. Yale Center for British Art, Paul Mellon Collection.

the margins of Tudor dynastic portraiture is certainly difficult to ignore, but also mysterious. He just stands there, as if
his mere presence was enough.

Distanced from the previous portraits but relevant to his
posthumous role is the image of Somer that perhaps has been
most widely distributed. It is an engraving by the artist Francis
Delaram that was sold as a single sheet by the printer Thomas
Jenner from about 1620 (fig. 7). Although the depiction of
Somer here is mainly imaginary, there are points of comparison with the earlier pictures that make it well worth a closer
look. In an insightful article on this print, theatre historian
John Astington observes how Somer's clothes and general
appearance here owe more to the theatrical representation of
him around the turn of the seventeenth century than to the
real Somer. He is here kitted out in Jacobean fashion, and
Astington connects the clothes with the costumes made for
actors who played Somer in Elizabethan and Jacobean history plays.[11] Somer is standing in an elegant pose, looking
hardly more like a comedian than he does in the earlier portraits, and in the background we see a townscape where
groups of children are playing various games, much like the
Bruegel painting *Children's Games* (1560).

But if we look more closely at his face, we see that it has
striking similarities with Somer's face in the Marian painting. Being a print, it is of course reversed, and at first sight the
features are not quite the same. But when we look at details
such as the placement of the collars, the silhouette of his
cheekbone, the lines on his face, and the general dimensions,
we see that the artist has probably worked from this painting,
a copy of it, or a lost original that formed the basis for the

FIGURE 7. *Will Sommers, king Heneryes Jester,* by Francis
Delaram, engraving c. 1620. Princeton University Art
Museum, J. S. Morgan Collection.

FIGURE 8. Comparison of figures 5 and 7.

extant painting as well (fig. 8). The curious result is that
Somer here looks even more menacing than he does in the
contemporary portraits, which is ironic, as the print surely
was made to capitalise on his celebrity as a comic figure. The
addition of a hat and a gold chain around his neck together
with his wide-legged posture gives him an air of dignity and
power that is not present in the older portraits. A comparison
with the psalter portrait underlines this with almost humourous emphasis. The image consequently visualises the meta-
morphosis that Somer has undergone from court fool to legendary comic.

Looking at Somer in the contemporary pictures, we cannot
avoid making some basic observations about his appearance
and what this might have signified. Although we are not here

to apply a modern diagnosis to Somer, and it will be virtually impossible to say anything about his mental status, a few speculative remarks on his physicality are relevant in order to see how his surroundings might have viewed him.

Somer's most notable physical feature, visible in all contemporary portraits, is his protruding forehead and brow ridge. In the court accounts, the ordering of handkerchiefs for him is understood by J. R. Mulryne as "intended for wiping nose and mouth to deal with a natural condition or illness" and by David Wiles as "needed to mop his saliva."[12] But the visual evidence hardly verifies this image of a drooling fool. The interpretation is refuted by Southworth, who thinks the quality of the handkerchiefs' fabric rules out this form of usage, opting instead for a possible "propensity for catching colds in the now ageing fool."[13] Somer's facial features are distinctive, certainly, but they hardly show signs of anything that would have been grounds for his employment.

Another feature visible in all extant portraits of Somer is that his hair is closely cropped—and always uncovered—in a way that stands out from most other male heads in Tudor portraits.[14] Although his head is never actually clean shaved, as asserted by some commentators, it does bring to mind the practice of shaving the heads of fools in this period. Jane Foole's head is probably shaved in the 1545 painting, though it is partly covered by a headdress. Anu Korhonen remarks that the shaven head of the fool could have many implications—his questionable masculinity (if the fool was a man), a sign of humiliation, or merely to attain a comic look—but primarily she suggests a medical reason for the baldness. Considered within the framework of humoural theory, in which the balance of bodily fluids is the key to good health, hair could be seen as obstructing "harmful vapours" from leaving the body. If it did, it was believed that memory would risk deteriorating, and memory was an essential part of the conception of folly at this time. Thus, Korhonen contends, "shaving off one's hair could be a treatment, if not cure, for simplicity and stupidity."[15] The question is why one would wish to alleviate stupidity in a person cherished for exactly that quality. But perhaps it was still considered necessary in order to "tame" the fool's folly.[16]

Turning to the matter of his dress, we firstly see that in nearly all depictions he is wearing green. Numerous entries in the wardrobe accounts of orders for green items of clothing for him might be taken as examples of this. Apart from those quoted in the previous chapter, we might take the 1555 order for the furring of a gown of green velvet and a jerkin of the same fabric, and in another entry a few months later, a payment for the making of two more green coats.[17] By the time of Somer's employment, the livery of servants at Henry's court had been established as green and white, usually in the shape of a green doublet and white jacket.[18] There is some visual evidence that this was accompanied by a pair of red or pink hose, in which case the uniform corresponds with Somer's dress in the 1545 family portrait. The shade of green of his doublet in that picture is different, however, from the most emphatically green dress he is shown wearing in any image—namely, the psalter illumination. The overall picture of the wardrobe accounts and the portraits indicates that the colour green had a special significance throughout Somer's time as a fool. In at least the psalter and Marian painting, and perhaps also the Boughton House portrait, he is wearing a hooded coat—green in the first two, brown in the third. In the 1545 family portrait, he is wearing a green doublet with narrow red stripes. In both this and the psalter, the same purse appears to be tied to his waist.[19] Some of the clothes ordered for Jane Foole were made of the same fabric used in clothes for Somer, which might mean that they appeared together in matching dress.

Previous commentators have emphasized that court fools of the sixteenth century, including Somer, never wore what was called a motley, the patchy multicoloured attire associated with fools in visual depictions. Wiles identifies this as a continental emblematic tradition that did not have any impact on English customs at this time, nor did it reflect how actual domestic fools dressed.[20] The same applies to the cockscomb headdress and the bauble, often attributes of the generic fool of paintings and illuminations. Although there might be some indications that fools in the fourteenth and fifteenth centuries wore this type of dress, and that it was worn in ceremonial occasions on the continent, it was definitely nonexistent in Tudor England, only to be picked up in a sort of nostalgic retro trend in the seventeenth century.[21] Indeed, none of the most famous court fools of the Renaissance, such as the French Triboulet (1479–1536), the German Claus Narr (1455–1530), the Florentine dwarf Morgante (second half of the sixteenth century), or the Spanish Perejón (mid-sixteenth century), were ever depicted in this type of extravagant clothes; instead, they were universally rendered in rather conventional, even toned-down clothes, as if their deviance would be apparent anyway.[22]

To modern eyes, Somer's dress does not single him out as different from other people at this time, but the basic features mentioned—the simplicity of his dress, the green colour, and bare head—would have been sufficiently clear signals to his contemporaries that he was neither a courtier nor an ordinary servant. Although green in the sixteenth century was often associated with positive emotions such as hope, beauty, and joy, it was also symbolic of envy through the belief that "envy built up bile, which gave the skin a distinctive green hue."[23] Green clothing also carried connotations of Robin Hood made apparent in numerous Robin Hood plays throughout the sixteenth century.[24] The colour was not unique for this particular fool, however. If we widen our gaze, we find green clothes on the Spanish court fool Calabacillas in Velazquez's portrait of him in the 1630s;[25] on Elisabet, the court fool of Anne of Hungary in the portrait by Jan van Hemessen, circa 1530; and on an anonymous court dwarf in Juan van der Hamen's portrait of 1626. In his classic account of the motley of Shakespeare's fool characters, Leslie Hotson asserts that green was very much the colour of the Renaissance fool.[26] But it is difficult to connect a certain colour to a narrowly defined symbolism in this period, and green had discrepant connotations. Erika Lin notes that "whereas livery in the household context clearly defined social role and status, in both the festive and theatrical contexts it signaled shifting and ephemeral identities."[27] Green clothes on fools is not a widespread enough practice to be considered customary. In fact, it is equally easy to find portraits of fools in red.[28]

Nostalgia was rife in the Henrician court, and it is tempting to see in Somer's greenness a reference to popular tradition, considering the role Somer would eventually come to play in pamphlets and jestbooks after his death. But while an Elizabethan and Jacobean context certainly connected the fool with a sentimental image of merry old England, an earlier period would not have been quite so explicit. To the Tudors, as to us, green was the colour of nature, and together with the plainness of his dress, it might be taken to symbolise the natural nature of the natural fool.[29] But perhaps the modesty is more important than the colour. In the end, then, it is hardly Somer's clothes or his exterior in these portraits that tells us something of his person or his role. Rather, it is the unassuming and inconspicuous nature of his appearances, the fact that he simply crops up, in the background or even foreground, and then just stands there, doing very little. There is nothing to suggest his foolery—no bells, no bauble, no juggling balls or musical instrument. There is only the man himself. And it must have been a man whose very presence spoke volumes to those in the know. Fools in other portraits smiled, pulled faces, showed their backsides. Not Somer. A faint smirk is the extent of his performance. An expression that seems to say to us, "Who am I?"

CHAPTER 7

Traits

THE FIRST glimpse we get of William Somer in any document that is not an administrative record from the court is in an early dramatic text. It is a brief interlude that was performed in the 1520s or '30s before an audience of members of the royal court—or at least of people associated with it. It was written by a promising young poet and singer, John Heywood, who would go on to become one of the most prolific and well-known writers of the Tudor age. The manuscript of the interlude is dated 1544, but it is generally believed to have been written some time earlier.[1] If *Witty and Witless*, as the interlude is generally called nowadays, was written before 1533, as the chief authorities on Heywood, Peter Happé and Greg Walker, would have it, then it constitutes the earliest known reference to Somer in writing after his introduction at court.

The interlude is a simple dialogue between two men called John and James, who enter the stage in the middle of a discussion on who is happier—the witty or the witless. Scholars are undecided on whether the beginning of the text is missing or whether Heywood intended it to start in medias res. As it is, John immediately begins the debate by denouncing the provocative statement that his interlocutor has just expressed: "Better to be a foole then a wyse man." James defends his position by comparing the witty, who are forced to fend for themselves in the world and make a living on their own, with the "naturall foole calde or thydeote," who in his reliance on other people's charity is liberated "from all kyndes of labore that dothe payne constrayne." John then tries to illustrate the hard life of fools by listing all the abuses they have to put up with:

Some beate hym, some bob hym
Some joll hym, some job hym,
Some tugg hym by the heres [arse],
Some lugg hym by the eares,
Some spet at hym, some spurne hym,
Some tosse hym, some turne hym,
Some snape hym, some snatche hym,
Some crampe hym, some cratche hym,
Some cuff, some clowt hym,
Some lashe hym, some lowte hym,
Some whysk hym, some whype hym,
Wythe scharpe naylys some nype hym,
Not evyn mayster Somer, the Kyngs gracys foole,
But tastythe some tyme some nyps of new schoole.[2]

Historian Pamela Allen Brown, among others, uses this list as one of the primary documentations of what she terms "Bad Fun," the cruel sort of humour and mockery that many claim to have haunted early modern culture in general and the professional life of kept fools in particular.[3] The addition of Somer's name at the end indicates of course that not even a fool of the king could escape this maltreatment, but this picture is altered when Somer is once more invoked, about halfway through the drama.

By now, James has unexpectedly won John over, but when John finally proclaims "better be a foole then a wyse man sewre," on to the stage walks a third character called Jerome, who replaces James in order to make things right and per-suade John to come back to reason. Jerome tries to explain that the witless man is equal to the animal, whereupon John interjects: "The sott hathe a resonabyll sowle, beasts have none." Jerome protests that "wytt of the sowle" is of no matter to the witless because they do not use it anyway. John con-cedes that the witless and the beast are "as one," and Jerome continues:

> Then schall thes beasts, wyttles man and myllhors, draw on
> Bothe yn one yoke: for thynke yow the nomber
> Standthe as Somer dothe all day yn slomber?
> Nay, Somer is a sot, foole for a kynge,
> But sots in many other mens howsyng
> Beare water, beare woodde, and do yn drugery
> In kychyn, cole howse, and in the norsery.
> And dayly for fawtes whyche they cannot refrayne,
> Evyn lyke the myll hors, they be whyppyd amayne.[4]

Now it is as if the equivalence of Somer and other maltreated fools is forgotten, and Somer stands apart from "sots in other men's housing" who are burdened with chores and whipped daily. Most modern editions of the text insert an exclamation mark after "sot" in the line "Nay! Somer is a sot! fool for a king!" but the exclamation mark is not in the original manuscript. Happé and Axton's 1991 edition substitutes a comma for the exclamation mark, but this is also an addition. The nominal phrase "sot fool for a king," without either exclamation mark or comma, might be read as a description of Somer's position. He is not merely a "sot," which could be taken to mean any person of mental deviance or disability, but a "sot fool"—that is, a sot who is employed as a fool. And not just anyone's sot fool, but a sot fool for a king! Heywood's use of the word "sot" has often been interpreted as a sign of his low opinion of Somer, and this perspective is reinforced as Jerome continues to speak:

> Other fooles that labor not have other conseyts:
> Uppon thydyll [th'idle] foole the flocke ever more
>   weytes.
> They tos hym, they turne hym, he is jobd and jolde,
> Whythe frettyng and fewmyng as ye a fore tolde:
> Excepte mayster Somer, of sotts not the best,
> But the myllhors may compare wythe hym for rest
> The[re]for plesewr conceyvyng or receyvyng,
> The wyttles and myllhors are bothe as one thyng.[5]

The rather clear statement that Somer is "of sots not the best" has been read literally as an expression of Heywood's dismissive attitude towards the court fool, and the reiteration of his laziness drives home the point. Heywood's depiction of Somer suggests that he was not primarily a performing fool. Indeed, the only trait or conduct that is connected to him here is his propensity for falling asleep. In the same breath as

Jerome disparages Somer, he refutes what was said earlier, that even Somer is occasionally treated cruelly or violently. All of a sudden, the tossing and turning, jobbing and jolling, fretting and fuming wreaked upon "idle fools" is not applicable to Master Somer. But perhaps Heywood is referring to a different type of treatment. The word "flock,"[6] taken together with the word "idle" here, might indicate that Jerome is speaking of unemployed fools who are subject to taunts and bullying by people in the street. In this collective, then, Somer is certainly an exception, since he lives a sheltered life behind castle walls. His resemblance to the mill-horse only applies to when the mill-horse is resting.

This passage, then, does not exactly undermine what was said about the treatment of fools in the beginning of the play, but simply that Somer, even though he is on occasion "nipped," is better off than other fools. And, in Heywood's opinion, perhaps better off than he deserves to be. Both Fairholt and Farmer conclude from Heywood's portrayal of Somer that the fool was a thorn in his side.[7] And it is easy to discern an underlying jealousy of the privileged position of the "sot fool" who has done little (?) to deserve it. In fact, Heywood concludes the entire piece by stating outright that "I hartyly wysche for encrese of rewarde" and that he hopes the king will in the future prefer "the wytty wyse wurker . . . Above thydyll sot."[8] Jeanne McCarthy reads these lines, in conjunction with impressions gained from Revels accounts, as Henry preferring pageantry and masking to watching plays.[9] Whether plays were already such an established contender for the attention of the monarch is open to question, but Heywood certainly expresses a hope that the king will opt for his type of entertainment and abandon his taste in "witless" fooling. Given this coda, it would not be unfitting to read the entire play as an invective against the taste for the "witless" comedy of natural fools, in favour of a more literary and intellectual style of comedy represented by Heywood.

It must surely have been aggravating that while poets and courtiers bent over backwards to gain favour, a man like Somer was in constant favour simply for being a fool. If such was the case, Heywood's jealousy is understandable. Although Somer is a privileged fool, he is here categorised as an idle fool who "labours not." His absence from records of performances is telling, but so is the absence of any sign that he should be a landed gentleman who did not need to work. The impression gained from Heywood's references to him is of a fool who was no entertainer or comedian. But in that case he must have been a treasured favourite of the king, and if the king was present at the performance of this play, as is often presumed, then what did he think of Heywood's ill-mannered depiction of his beloved fool?[10] If Heywood was eager to gain favour, it would have been very unwise to slander the king's fool. So perhaps dismissing the fool was not fraught with risk? We should remember the opening remark, that even Master Somer might taste "some nips of new school" now and then, which suggests that no fool was ever respected, and no king would be angry with a man who insulted his fool. Since Heywood was dismissed from regular court service as early as 1528, thereafter writing plays for the court on a more ad hoc basis, then maybe he was more inclined to speak freely. On the other hand, his connections with several enemies of Henry through his wife (including Thomas More, who was his wife's uncle, and whose relationship to the king deteriorated after 1530) might have made him more cautious.[11] In the end, the most plausible conclusion might be that Somer was an open target, even for poets whose relationship to the king was tenuous.

So what is the composite picture of "Master Somer" gained from Heywood's brief references to him? We learn that he was a favoured court fool, although not the most skilled, and on occasion he could be disciplined. In Heywood's eyes he was a "sot" (a foolish, stupid person). But the most distinctive trait that we obtain from Heywood's portrait is Somer's sleepiness. He stands "all day in slumber," and where other fools are comparable to the mill-horse in their drudgery, Somer is comparable to it in his rest. Heywood uses Somer's sleepiness to make claims about his lack of diligence and skill as a fool, but the straightforward way that this trait is presented makes it apparent that it is not just a matter of laziness. Somer really does sleep a lot. And if it had not been for Heywood's allusion to this, we would be forced to dismiss Robert Armin's account of this proclivity in his brief biography. Of all the anecdotes and claims about Somer in Armin's chapter on him in his *Foole upon Foole*, this is perhaps the most credible:

Will Sommers being in no little creadit in the kings court walking in the parke at Greenewich, fell a sleep on the stile that leades into the walke, and being many that would haue gone that way, so much loued him, that they were loath to disease him, but went an other way, I the better sort: but doe I make a wonder at that? who sooner then the better sort? for now a dayes beggers are the gallants, while Gentles of right bloud seeme tame ruffians: But note the loue that Will Sommers got: a poore woman seeing him sleep so daungerously, eyther to fall backward, or hurt his head leaning so against a poast, fetcht him a cushion and a rope, the one for his head, and the other to bind him to the poast for falling backward: and thus hee slept and the woman stood by, attending as grome of his chamber.[12]

We learn here more about his contemporaries and their attitude toward him than we do about Somer himself. Seeing him asleep on the stile, all the people who wanted to pass went in another direction so as not to wake him up. Armin's brief and somewhat confusing interjection about how even the better sort had this compassion, while nowadays gentlefolk are mere "tame ruffians," is typical of his chatty and informal style, but it adds a note of nostalgia that a modern reader might see as undermining the narrative's credibility. The action of the poor woman who became so worried he would fall over that she tied him down and gave him a cushion is endearing, and it sets the tone for the rest of Armin's portrayal of Somer. Inherent in this woman's attitude is the perception of the fool as a loveable man looked down on not as a slave or servant but as a child or pet. He instils a caring and considerate response in people, and it is presumed throughout that all who encounter him know who he is. This familiarity resounds in Heywood, and Somer comes across in both works as a sort of charm for the court, a harmless presence who infuses a perhaps much-needed slice of tranquility to court life through his incessant idleness and ability to sleep anywhere.

Whether Somer's somnolence was due to some medical condition or a personal disposition we shall never know.

Hilary Mantel makes it the basis for her brief snapshot of him in *The Mirror & the Light*, the last in her trilogy of Cromwell novels. Practically diagnosing him with narcolepsy, she writes that he "falls asleep while he is talking. He sits at table and slam goes his head, right down into his platter. He is not safe in the street; if he did not have a servant to check him he might fall under the wheels of a cart."[13] Sleepiness and laziness were recurring ingredients in early modern comedy, and they seem to have had complex connotations. Fundamentally, sleep had very negative implications from a religious point of view, recalling both Saint Paul's entreaty "Now is the time to awake out of sleep" as an admonition against a neglect of Scripture, and the deadly sin of sloth, which was strongly linked to a sluggish mind and a surrendering to the influence of the devil. The later famed clown character of Falstaff would be intimately linked to sleep, being first presented asleep in *Henry IV, Part I*, and placing a pillow on his head for a crown when impersonating Prince Hal's father.[14] The medieval aligning of folly and sin meant that the seven deadly sins especially were noted as markers of folly, and fools in theatre or literature could be used to embody sins.[15] Sleeping men and women are perpetually tricked in jestbooks from the sixteenth and seventeenth centuries, illustrating how sleep signalled a lack of awareness and control. But there was a wider association also, linking sleep to mental lethargy and physical ailments. Falstaff laments the king's apoplexy, calling it "a kind of lethargy . . . a kind of sleeping in the blood," mirroring how Renaissance writers viewed external behaviour and internal conditions as complementary.[16] And anything that implied lethargy could potentially be linked to folly and the possession of a "dull mind." Thus it might be that anyone suffering from a condition causing drowsiness, or who was generally considered lazy, ran the risk of being considered a fool, at the same time that laziness and falling asleep at inopportune moments might have been encouraged as an amusing trait in an employed fool.

"The life of the natural fool could well sound rather grim and pointless," says Anu Korhonen, "but this was by no means the case." As she considers how Renaissance culture imbued the fool with positive meanings, she concludes that "they were also happy, as they lived without worry."[17] Since Christian doctrine of the period often considered natural fools as closer to God through their simplicity and childlike inability to sin, it urged people to treat them with compassion, and the early modern keeping of fools was often seen as a form of charity. But, as we have seen, fools were also seen as deficient human beings and their stupidity an easy bait for demonic influence.[18] In morality plays and woodcuts, fools were depicted as little devils. Therefore, it was alright to laugh at them.[19] From Somer's tendency to fall asleep, or at least the view of him by others that he spent "all day in slumber," we glimpse the courtly encouragement of traits that underpinned his role as a fool. These traits were often of a kind that were forbidden for anyone who wished to appear civilised or dignified, but that were comfortable and relaxing to anyone who indulged in them. Castiglione, in his *Book of the Courtier*, which was translated into English by Thomas Hoby in 1561, discourages his readers from trying to arouse laughter in the way that fools did:

> For undoubtedlye it is not meete for a Gentlemanne to make weepinge and laughing faces, to make sounes and

voices, and to wrastle with himselfe alone as Berto doeth, to apparaile himself like a lobb of the Countrey as doeth Strascino, and such other matters, which do well beecome them, bicause it is their profession. But we must by the way and privilie steale this counterfeiting, alwayes keeping the astate of a gentilman, without speaking filthy wordes, or doing uncomelye deedes, without making faces and antiques, but frame our gestures after a certein maner, that who so heareth and seeth us, may by our wordes and countenances imagin muche more then he seeth and heareth, and upon that take occasion to laughe.[20]

His references to the Sienese clown Strascino and the papal fool Berto likely passed over the heads of English readers, but the ambition towards courtly mannerisms that were in vogue and had certainly reached the English court well before the printing of Hoby's translation makes it quite clear that courtiers could not allow themselves to be as relaxed and as forthright as court fools.[21] It is quite unproblematic to conclude that Tudor courtiers were not perfectly relaxed while appearing at court—especially not, perhaps, in the presence of the king. But was the unpredictable and limitless behaviour of the court fool a universal thing? Tales of Italian fools, like those of the infamous Gonnella of the ducal court at Ferrara, tell of men who could roam free within the castle walls, subjecting anyone at any time to a cruel practical joke (such as, in the case of the Ferrarese royal physician, taking a strong laxative and sitting on someone's face while they were asleep).[22] There is no recorded story of Somer doing anything like that, and if he had that inclination, surely anecdotes of such shenanigans would have been left behind in some form or another. Not even in the late jest biography of him, so full of stock jokes and anecdotes, is there a tale of any pugnacious or scatological pranking. Whether or not such events took place at court was clearly conditioned by the personality of the resident fool—and presumably the licence given to him by his employer. What fools could and could not do differed between courts all over Europe during the several centuries when fools were a common feature.

Will Somer's sleepiness, however, is linked to this licence in that it is a sign of what made the fool a fool at Henry's court, and what might have been an encouraged or cherished quality. It allows us to imagine Somer in the context of the court, not running around like a wild trickster, but rather milling about languidly, like an old dog or a cat. The care with which he is treated in the story of his falling asleep on the gate suggests how the people of the court looked down on him as an inferior at the same time that they felt affection for him. There are decidedly echoes here of Tuan's pet theory. But to other people connected to the court, such as John Heywood, who tried to make a career and gain favour, the presence of a fool who could be forgiven for sleeping in the royal chambers was likely an eyesore. It is hardly surprising, then, that Heywood relishes in the physical punishment Somer also has to endure.

But how does this tally with the picture of a fool who may sleep when and where he wishes? To be fair, Heywood first sets Somer apart from other fools who are routinely beaten, saying that Somer *in spite of this* sometimes cannot escape physical punishment. It says more, perhaps, about the general treatment of fools than that the treatment of Somer was particularly harsh. In the years after his death, there was an anecdote circulating about him that reveals another side to the aggressive atmosphere surrounding the fool. The anecdote crops up occasionally in publications from the decades following his death, but the earliest occurrence I have found is from Somer's lifetime. Roger Ascham, the didactic writer and royal administrator, mentions the anecdote in his book *Toxophilus* (1545). The work, which was dedicated to Henry VIII, advocates a certain type of archery, and in doing so, has reason to mention the king's fool:

> Of those that blame shotinge and shoters, I wyll saye nomore at this tyme but this, that beside that they stoppe and hinder shoting, which the kinges grace wolde haue forwarde, they be not moche vnlyke in this poynt to Wyl Somer the king his foole, which smiteth him that standeth always before his face, be he neuer so worshipfull a man, and neuer greatly lokes for him whiche lurkes behinde an other man his back, that hurte him in dede.[23]

In later versions, this would be abbreviated to an almost proverbial form, as when Brian Melbancke in his *Philotimus* (1583) remarks, "Thou arte moste like Will Summer, which being hurte with anye, thoughe he stoode a Furlonge of him, woulde always strike his nexte fellowe."[24] It was similarly used in the Elizabethan period by both Thomas Lodge and John Harington, but the fact that it is referred to by Ascham, who was close to the court, strongly suggests a basis in fact.[25] To Ascham it is a suitable parable for anyone who puts the blame for something in the wrong place, and thus it might be a saying that appropriates the name of a then current individual to make it more relatable. It is not a saying, however, that to my knowledge has been connected to any other fool, and it corresponds with other indications about Somer's personality.

There are vague suggestions in Somer's posthumous reputation that he had a violent temper. We have already had reason to quote the anecdote in the 1637 jest biography of how he quarrelled with a man who called him a liar, threatening him with a cudgel. Both this tale and Gabriel Harvey's reference to Somer in 1593 as "the chollericke foole" are highly tenuous sources of knowledge on Somer's personality, but seen in the light of Ascham's story, they might be vestiges of his reputation for outbursts.[26] Although the 1637 tale ends with Somer suddenly not carrying out the punishment with which he threatens his opponent, there is much emphasis on Somer's known temper, his antagonist "knowing his suddennesse, and that he was but a word and a blow."[27] He was, however, not the only fool of his age with such a reputation. I have previously mentioned Richard Tarlton's documented bouts of rage, and Robert Armin tells in his compendium of fool biographies of the fool Lean Leanard, an extreme example who in one anecdote winds himself up in such a rage that he throws stools and glasses about himself and books into the fire. The rest of the household becomes so concerned at the noise that they are forced to break open the door to his chamber, and when they finally enter they find the fool has brutally assaulted himself— "his pate broken his face scratcht, and legge out of joynt."[28] The cause for the rage was a game of shuffleboard that he played with himself.

Armin does not represent Somer as quite so violent and aggressive. He gives him the epithet "merry fool," but, as noted, he relates how Somer once avenged a rival jester by throwing a bowl of pudding at his head. Few fools, it seems, did not at some point find themselves in a confrontational situation, which perhaps says more about the conditions of their occupation than their mental state. While a fool like Lean Leanard comes across as an unstable and violent person in all anecdotes about him, Ascham's story about Somer does not portray him in quite the same light. Somer's tendency to strike the man standing closest to him instead of the man who actually slandered him suggests the behaviour of a man with some form of neurosis or intellectual disability when put under extreme pressure. It is thus easier to believe Ascham's story about Somer's misdirected blow than the jest biography's tale about Somer's threatening behaviour. Ascham's story sticks out more than a simple anecdote about an argument that honestly could have been about anybody. It is particularly interesting in that it both records an instance of Somer's behaviour and shows how those relating it saw in it the potential for a useful parable, if not quite a jest.

Ascham uses the anecdote, comprised to a single statement, only to dismiss those who scoff at archery as a whole in view of the malpractice of a few unskilled shooters. The inclusion of the reference to Somer has nothing to do with the topic of the text itself. By introducing the word "always," Ascham's way of phrasing it turns something that might have happened once into a general conduct, a typical feature of how gossip about a person works—from "he once hit the man standing closest to him when someone else abused him" to "that's the man who hits whoever is closest to him when someone abuses him."[29] When Ascham wrote *Toxophilus* he was a shunned Cambridge scholar eagerly in search of patronage.

He wrote his book on archery and dedicated it to the king, knowing full well of his interest in the pastime.[30] By invoking the king's fool in his oration on archery, he strikes a familiar note, perhaps hoping to appeal to the king through recognisable topics. In this endeavour, it would be risky of him to refer to a rumour about Somer that could be a fiction. If he wanted the king and his close circle to read it, he needed to get his facts straight, especially on things that the king would have firsthand knowledge of. By mentioning Somer's tendency to strike impulsively, Ascham thus speaks directly to the king and his closest men as if in candid conversation with them. The straightforward phrasing of the sentence—Somer, "which smiteth him that standeth always before his face"—makes it beyond doubt that this is what he does. There is no "whom I have heard smiteth" or "who is said to smite."

In this way, the phrasing does not really allude to an incident so much as a general tendency—a volatility or lack of restraint. The tetchy Somer contrasts with the languid somnambulist of Heywood's and Armin's depictions, but other references to him show him in a similar light. In one of the belligerent pamphlets of the religious controversialist and clergyman John Bale, published in 1552, a lengthy malicious portrait of a Catholic priest culminates in an account of how this man reads from the scripture in a "stuttering and stammering" manner:

> More apysh toyes & gawdysh feates, could neuer a dysarde [fool] in England haue plaied (I think) than that apysh prest shewed there at the cōmunyon. He turned and tossed, lurked and lowted, snored and smirted, gaped and

gasped, kneled and knocked, loked and lycked, with both his thombes at hys eares & other tryckes more, that he made me, xx, tymes to remembre wylle Somer, Yet of them both, that prest semed y^t more foole a great deale.[31]

Somer is here used to liken the depicted priest to a fool, not by equating what this man says to the foolish things fools say, but by comparing the priest's conduct to that of Somer, emphasising the fool's apparent quivering and nervous disposition—turning and tossing, stuttering and stammering, kneeling and knocking—along with other, more elusive qualities. "Lurking" and "lowting" are words that could have multiple meanings, but most commonly they denoted sneaking or stealing about in a furtive manner. "Smirting" is related to smarting, to speak hurtfully, but when coupled with "snoring" it seems mainly to characterise the man's voice. Some of the verbs used here are probably meant to portray the priest rather than Somer, but the general impression of the list is meant to embody the fool. The picture is one of trembling and fidgeting, thereby suggesting a neurotic or spasmodic person. Two words that stand out say perhaps other things: "snoring" conjures up the familiar image of drowsiness, and "licking" might indicate a nervous tic or compulsion, or be related to Somer's noted need for handkerchiefs.

This list of words coupled with Ascham's reference provides us with a sketchy picture. It does not allow us to deem whether the man we see is disabled or neurotic, but the diagnosis is irrelevant. What we can vaguely discern is an image. Together with the extant portraits we can conjure up an apparition of him. This allows us to draw some limited conclusions about what might have placed him in the position of court fool in the first place. But it also reveals some unattractive aspects about what was laughed at and how a man like him might have been treated. Alongside the care and compassion perceptible in the sleeping-on-the-gate scene, it is hard to ignore the impression that Somer could also be laughed at and taunted. It seems that such taunting would often be perpetrated with the intention of producing an amusing reaction that could be related as an anecdote by those witnessing it, and consequently spread among people connected to the court. But were such anecdotes categorised as comedy in the modern sense of the word, or should they instead be considered oral mythology with a wider purpose, encouraging reflection just as much as laughter?

Up until the days of the Elizabethan stage clowns, access to performing comics was reserved for a select few. There were certainly travelling players during the entire Middle Ages, but their performances would have been irregular, and it is uncertain to what extent their comic performers constituted a distinct category. Fools outside of courts and noble households appear to have been identical to what in modern times have been called "village idiots" or "local characters"—men and women who stood out because of a disability or some form of eccentricity and who were considered amusing because of it. Even in modern times, such persons were figures of folklore just as much as—or even more than—real individuals, and their idiosyncrasies are often difficult to disentangle from the many local myths about them, which is also the case with persons from the recent past. Thus they became figures of fun in the oral sphere, the stories about them living a life of their own and composing a biography and a character that was separate from the man or woman providing the inspiration for them. Such mythological figures were important in the rural or illiterate spheres of society in the nineteenth and twentieth centuries, and were probably even more so in the early modern period.[32]

Thus, in an age when physical access to comic performers was scarce for many, comedians were a group of people who lived in the oral realm rather than the physical. Only when the establishment of permanent theatres created a more concrete and accessible form of entertainment was it possible for the profession of clown to develop and performed comedy to acquire the nuances necessary for an eventual division into highbrow and lowbrow forms. That later period played a large role in shaping the modern concept of comedy as something lightweight and relieving, rather than challenging or provoking. Looking at early Elizabethan drama, for instance, the clowns are much more chaotic and riotous—and inevitably more difficult for modern viewers to find funny—than the increasingly shrewd and parodic clowns of the Jacobean and later eras.[33] The more violent degradation and humiliation directed at medieval fools also cast them in the role of an outlet or religious symbol rather than a comic.[34] So we might carry with us the hypothesis that comedy in Somer's time was still not as much about wit and relief as in later periods, and was more about parable and mirroring. This might help us appreciate the role that Somer played and what it was that kept him in royal favour for so long.

CHAPTER 8

Words

PERHAPS THE clearest example of what could be called either
William Somer's "wit" or his foolishness is found in a reference
to him by the scholar and administrator Thomas Wilson in his
1553 *The Arte of Rhetorique.* It is probably the most quoted joke
attributed to Somer, but there have been few attempts to dis-
sect it. Wilson's book is divided into small sections, each deal-
ing with a rhetorical device. Under the heading "Alteryng parte
of a worde" we find the following passage:

> Altering parte of a worde, is when we take a letter or sill-
> able from some worde, or els adde a letter, or sillable to a
> worde. As thus. William Somer seeing much adoe for ac-
> comptes making, and that the Kinges Maiestie of most
> worthie memorie Henrie the eight wanted money, such as
> was due vnto him: and please your grace (quoth he) you
> haue so many Frauditours, so many Conueighers, and so
> many Deceiuers to get vp your money, that they get all to
> themselues. Whether he sayd true or no, let God iudge
> that, it was vnhappely spoken of a foole, and I thinke he

had some Schoolemaster: He should haue saide Auditours, Surueighours, and Receiuers.[1]

The quotation of Somer is often taken as an example of an astute comic deliberately mispronouncing the words "auditors," "surveyors," and "receivers" to imply that the officials involved in the royal finances—the auditors who examined and verified accounts, the surveyors who calculated the value of property, and the receiver, or treasurer, in charge of collecting payments—are deceptive and fraudulent.[2] Wilson adds a few caveats, however, which complicate matters. His first reservation—amounting to "whether he spoke truly or not is not for me to say"—is straightforward enough and indicates that Wilson wishes to dissociate himself from the biting remark in order to avoid blame. He underlines his stance by condemning the fool's words—"unhappily" in this context should probably be read in the sense of "mischievously" or "maliciously," a meaning that was commonly ascribed to the word in the sixteenth century. But it is what he says thereafter that is the most interesting: "I thinke he had some Schoolemaster." This can be read in various ways. A modern reader might interpret Wilson's words as saying, "Somer was not that uneducated." But more likely, Wilson is suggesting that Somer was coached, or "schooled," by someone to say what he did.[3]

It is difficult to believe that Somer would indeliberately, through sheer stupidity, have altered these three words into three other words in a way that gave the saying a deeper critical meaning. But evidently Wilson is reluctant to think that Somer could have been clever enough to concoct this joke on his own. There seems to have been some ambiguity in the gossip of the court concerning Somer's foolery. Utterances like the one Wilson quotes circulated as proof of Somer's shrewdness, but at the same time a sense of uncertainty surrounded him. In a poem written around the time of Somer's death, Thomas Churchyard refers to "the Renowmed Rhetoricien willm Somer" with blatant irony.[4] Was it difficult to square quotations like the one about the king's auditors with the man himself to those who had met him? Or was Wilson mainly concerned with defending the fool's reputation?

Another aspect of Wilson's references to Somer is his discreet way of indicating his familiarity with him. His doubts about the true origins of the quotation signal to his readers that he was close by when it was uttered. As with John Heywood's reference to Somer, the fool functions as a useful motif to be taken up by those who wish to gain favour at court, but in both instances the reference is equivocal. Wayne Rebhorn has observed that Thomas Wilson wrote his book on rhetoric when he was in the initial stages of his career, and that his allusions to fools and jesters betray a conflicted attitude toward the popular culture connected to the humble background from which he tried to distance himself.[5] His career as a scholar at Cambridge and tutor in noble households did not take off until after the death of Henry VIII in 1547. He tutored the children of the Duchess of Suffolk and the Duke of Northumberland and became part of the circle of academics that had connections in high places, including the aforementioned Roger Ascham and John Cheke, who was tutor to Edward VI. In the early 1550s, Wilson wrote his two best-known works, *The Arte of Rhetorique* and *The Rule of Reason*. It is probably during these years of close contact with men in noble and royal circles that he became aware of and possibly even met Will Somer. After the accession of Mary in 1553, Wilson was one of the many Protestants who fled the land, and so his knowledge and associations with the court must have preceded that. Wilson's references to Somer confirm this. He would not return to England until 1560, after Somer's death.

The quoted passage from *Arte of Rhetorique* is not the first instance where Somer's name is invoked in the book. A few pages earlier, Wilson berates various fashionable attempts by men of lesser learning to appear more learned by using Latinisms in their language. The label of "inkhorn terms" had become popular among writers to denote such linguistic flamboyance. "I knowe them that thynke Rhetorique, to stande wholy vpon darke woordes," begins Wilson, "and he that can catche an ynke horne terme by the taile, hym thei compt to bee a fine Englishe man, and a good Rhetorician. And the rather to set out this folie, I will adde here suche a letter, as Willyam Sommer himself, could not make a better for that purpose."[6] Here Somer is brought into play simply as a representative of his occupation, but it is noteworthy that Wilson should repeatedly mention him in connection with linguistic and rhetorical foolishness. Does this mean that Somer was known for his garbling of language as exemplified in his "mispronunciation" of the account makers? If so, there remains an ambivalence of whether this tendency was a sign of his stupidity or of his skill with language. But it is striking how uninterested Wilson is in resolving this ambivalence.

In Wilson's other great work, *The Rule of Reason*, first published in 1551, there is no mention of Somer. But in the third edition of 1553—the same year as *Arte of Rhetorique* was first printed—an anecdote concerning a fool has been inserted. The reference to this fool is similar in style to that of the other book, but it gives us a more unpolished example of his discourse. In the chapter entitled "The places of false conclusions, or deceiptfull reasons," Wilson discourses at one point on the role of double meanings in logical disputations, whereupon he interjects:

> A certaine person, that is no small foole, as al menne ful wel knowe, that knowe him at all, beeing earnest at a time, in commending a Bishoppe of his acquaintaunce, declared to a noble personage, that this Bishoppe had a goodlie base voice, and made at one time (quoth he) as base a Sermone, as he neuer hearde the like in all his life before, and therefore, woorthie to be coumpted a great Clerke, in his foolish iudgemente. Who will not saie, that this Bishoppe was baselie praised.[7]

Although Wilson does not specify whom this concerns, the name "William Somar" is printed in the margin, and the reference has more of the nature of a repeated quote than the previous allusion. The comedy rests on the same phenomenon—the fool saying one thing but meaning something else—but here his gaffe does not consist of altering one word into another that gives the phrase a new meaning. Rather, he simply uses a word with two meanings in a way that gives his statement an unintended meaning. It is reminiscent of the way a child might use a word in the wrong way, being oblivious to how it could be found humourous by an adult, and it is implied here that Somer did not himself understand that he had made a gaffe. In transferring the word "base" from the initial use as descriptor of the bishop's voice to the second accidental use as descriptor of the sermon—and by extension the quality of the sermon—Somer thinks he has made a perceptive observation and his surroundings are laughing behind his back. Did he do this intentionally in order to be funny and to play the expected role of the fool? As we will see, he implicitly criticised the clergy at other occasions as well, but the statement is markedly different from the one in *Arte of Rhetorique* in that it can more easily be read as a simpleminded person's blunder. In that way, if taken as a verbatim documentation of the fool's saying, it is just as clever a piece of foolery as the remark about the king's accountants in that it disguises disparaging mockery in an apparently stupid slipup. The fool's well-known "licence" would only be accepted if the question of his actual folly remained unresolved. Perhaps it was a part of the game to go along with the fool's act.

Wilson sometimes appears to do so. Further emphasising his familiarity with the court, he says that those who "knowe [Somer] at all" know "ful wel" that he is "no small foole." Although he may have suspected that Somer was not as shrewd as some thought, he also had an interest in defending the fool as a means of pledging his own allegiance to the throne. It is difficult to determine whether it was all a game, but its elusive nature appears to have been the main feature of the game. Wilson certainly treats Somer condescendingly, holding him forth as a failed rhetorician, but the failures are given meaning. The quote by Somer is one of a long line of hidden religious criticisms in *Rule of Reason*. In many of the examples he gives of true and false logic, bishops become the target for implicit invective, especially in several illustrations of logical reasoning ending in the conclusion that bishops and priests should be allowed to marry. In the passage where he refers to Somer, Wilson also vilifies those who quarrel and dispute based on insufficient knowledge: "Scholars dispute, wise menne fall out, lawiers agree not. Preachers ware hotte, Gentlemen striue, the people mutter, good menne geue counsail, women haue their woordes, this manne affirmeth, the other denigheth, and yet at lengthe, the double meaning beeing ones knowen (when al thinges are quiete) endes the whole matter." The wisest person, concludes Wilson, is the man who in "seeing repugnaunte sentences, can by reason iudge the trueth."[8] William Somer, then, is a man who cannot discern between two meanings of a word using his reason, but in his foolish utterances lies fodder for criticisms that might be picked up by those around him.

Voicing controversial criticisms through the use of fools was a well-established literary practice by this time, as exemplified by the previously mentioned works of Brant and Erasmus.[9] As noted, Somer's name is invoked by several theological writers during the religious struggles surrounding the reigns of Henry, Edward, and Mary. The references to him are all quite curious and the reason for them not always clear. He is called on to support the arguments of both Catholic and anti-Catholic polemicists, implying a potential to imbue his words with whatever meaning the writer saw fit. A fiery but probably apocryphal reference is found in the Paris-based Franciscan Thomas Bourchier's 1582 history of Catholic martyrs. When telling the story of the death in 1537 of Thomas

Belchiam, a Franciscan imprisoned by Henry VIII, he relates
that "a certain madman, who from his birth was deprived of
the faculty of reason, by the name of William Sommer, went
running about the court shouting 'The simplicity of one men-
dicant breaks the pride of the King.' God perfects his praise
out of the mouths of infants and sucklings: by the new and
singular example of a fool, here God willed to accomplish his
praise."[10] Bourchier does his best to exploit this story of its
potential to make the fool a mouthpiece of God in a divine
condemnation of Henry. One might be tempted here to read
the absence of this anecdote from other writings as an attempt to hush up a critical comment on Henry made by his
own fool, but most likely it is a fiction. Bourchier curiously
writes as if Somer is completely unknown to him, or perhaps
he presents him this way because he is addressing a continental readership, to whom the name William Somer likely meant
nothing. Although of unknown origins, Bourchier lived in
England until the 1560s and studied at Oxford, which would
mean that he had time to acquaint himself with the celebrities
or gossip of the court. The direct link between Somer's alleged
outburst and the demise of an imprisoned Catholic is too
neat to be believable, but perhaps the story stems from a hazy
awareness of a fickle fool at Henry's court.

We see, of course, traces here of the belief that fools' words
were the undisguised truth, but such instances are most often
connected to mythical or fictional paradigms. The reality of
the expectations and interpretations of fools is slightly different. The nonsense bordering on insight that Bourchier attributes to Somer in this case is probably apocryphal, but it corresponds to other examples that are more vague and brief, but

also—and perhaps therefore—more credible. Another explicit, albeit unassuming, reference to Somer by a theological writer is found in a footnote in an English translation of a text by the Zurich-based Protestant reformer Rudolf Gwalther. That Gwalther is not the author of this footnote is quite evident, since, although he had contacts with English Calvinists during the Marian exile, he never visited England or had close dealings with the English court. Tales of William Somer could have reached him via exiled Englishmen, but it is unlikely. The English translation of Gwalther's viciously anti-Catholic pamphlet *Antichrist* (1556) was printed in the German town of Emden and secretly distributed in England.[11] Its translator is named on the title page as "I. O.," which almost certainly refers to the exiled priest John Old, active as translator in Emden at the time. He is also probably the source of the note that reads: "Cloisterers fratres in vnum knaues all quod william Somer."[12] The note is printed in the margin of a page that describes how "cloistre men" have become skilled in "scraping together" riches and land that could have fed thousands of people. Evidently the English translator here saw fit to insert a quotation that neatly summed up the gist of the argument.

It is interesting that Old should add the words "quod william Somer" at the end. If he had not, there would have been no point in appending the note, so clearly the allusion to the fool has meaning. That friars should be identified as knaves by a man who is himself a knave seems to be a reiteration of the well-worn modern phrase "It takes one to know one," versions of which might have been in circulation in early modern times.[13] Thus Somer's name is used here as a sort of authority

on identifying folly. At the same time, Somer is implicitly portrayed as a simpleton in making this crude and—within its
context—obvious statement. The sentence has a simplicity
and a comical plainness that is similar to some other sayings
attributed to Somer, so it is possible that Old here relates an
aphorism he has heard himself. He might of course have heard
others quote Somer, but the sentence is so short and simple
that it seems an insufficient subject matter for gossip. Unlike
the allusions to him in later books, the references made to
Somer while he was still living must be limited in the amount
of freedom they can take with their characterisation. Consequently, he comes across here in much the same light as in
Thomas Wilson's works—a natural fool that accidentally says
meaningful things, or who says stupid things that might later
be used to strengthen an argument. Somer may have been
cherished for just his tendency to do this, and the way writers
use his utterances indicates that the sayings of fools—or of
this particular fool—had a special function. Some historians
have argued that fools were kept partly for the clairvoyant
abilities they were thought to possess.[14] Such might have been
the case with some of the court dwarfs of seventeenth-century
Spain, but there is little to suggest this was the case with English court fools.[15] Rather, fools might have been valued for
their tendency to produce remarks that could be given meaning by observers after the fact.

   In several contemporary texts, William Somer is credited
with a phrase that illustrates quite well how his words were
taken up and given the status of a figure of speech despite
being seemingly plain. The earliest example I have found of
this is in a letter from the diplomat William Paget to Henry

VIII in December 1545. Paget was at the time private secretary to the king and one of the most powerful officeholders in the country. He was sent on several missions to France to negotiate a peace treaty after the English had besieged Boulogne, and it is in a letter from one of these trips that he incidentally mentions Somer:

> Finally, touching Your Majestie, thEmpereur, the French King, thAlmains, and every Princes Counseillours, I have praysed, dispraysed; given hope, feare, mistrust, jelouzie, suspicion, respectively. I have lyed, sayd trouth, spoken fayre, roughly, and plaisantly; promised giftes, pensions; and don all that may be don or sayd for thadvauncement of this mater, and moch more then I will abyde by (as William Somer sayth) if I wer asked the question. But all is in Goddes hande, and it is He, that, byyonde all mens expectations, and contrary to their opinions and devises, directeth thinges at His pleasure to His glory.[16]

It is not clear at first exactly what in this passage encompasses Somer's quote. Both Enid Welsford and John Southworth have quoted this letter as an illustration of Somer's wit, presumably taking the entire sentence to be a quotation from the fool.[17] But when comparing this letter with other documents that also refer to Somer, one is forced to adjust the scope of this promising find. A sentence in the priest John Proctor's book of religious criticisms four years later is revealing: "Or ye haue forgotten that whiche ye sayde in the beginninge of this your laste sentêce, or els ye use to say one thing & thinke an other, other els because ye wyll not be condemned in any thinge, ye wyll abyde by nothynge that ye say: and ths is a wyse touch q[uod] Wyll Somer."[18] In spite of his association with Oxford and scholars close to the court, Proctor's work controversially disparages Protestantism, but the subject of his pamphlet has little bearing on the brief reference to Somer.[19] The common denominator of this sentence and the passage in Paget's letter is one word used in conjunction with Somer's name—"abide."

A third allusion to Somer a few years later helps shed light on this. This time it is the diplomat Nicholas Wotton, writing to the secretary of state Sir William Petre in early 1554 on the business of the ensuing wedding between Queen Mary and Philip of Spain:

> I send you herewith a certain declaration, whereby may appear (as I take it) certain degrees of consanguinity and affinity wherein the Queen's Highness and the Prince of Spain are knit together. But I remember very well, that I have oftentimes heard my fellow Will Somer (God keep him warm, wheresoever he be!) say, that he would abide by no saying of his; and, forasmuch as it is ever good to learn of a wise man, I intend therefore, in this matter, to learn a lesson of him.[20]

With three brief quotations, we have now travelled from the last years of Henry's reign to the time of Mary Tudor. Many momentous political events are taking place in the background, but we shall remain focused on these three passing references to a fool. As we see, the name Will Somer is once more connected to the use of the word "abide," although all three men use this word in slightly varying phrases: "much more than I will abide by," "abide by nothing that you say," and "abide by no saying of his." The first two are concerned with one's own utterances, while the third changes focus and urges distrust against anything another person says. The curious recurrence of this reference to Somer shows us that he is credited with little more than the use of the word "abide."[21] What began as a promising documentation of the fool's rare wit thus ends up being an unremarkable quotation of at most a few words. Its connection to Somer lived on for some time after his death, as confirmed by Bishop John Bridges's reiteration of it in one of his books as late as 1573: "But if ye *put the case* (as ye say) like *Master Dorman*, then dare ye not abide, by this case neither lyke Wylliam Sommer, for so playde *Master Dorman* in *putting this case*, and so I feare in the ende ye must be fayne to do."[22]

But perhaps the words are more revealing than they seem. In its most elementary sense, the phrase states that you shouldn't hold to any claim or promise made by a fool. With a little imagination, it amounts to virtually the same message as that of the famous line commonly attributed to Groucho Marx: "I don't care to belong to any club that will have me as a member."[23] Although it has been suggested that this joke predates Marx, it is difficult to trace it back to the time of Will Somer. The gist of Somer's line is that the fool expresses self-conscious doubt about the veracity or validity of anything uttered by a fool. But it can imply doubt about both the fool's sincerity and his sanity, just as Marx's joke implies doubt about both his sincerity and his character. The question is whether this was an archetypal motto of fools or whether it actually came from Somer's mouth. That so many attribute it to Somer can mean either that he coined the phrase or that he was *the* fool to all who referred to one in Tudor England, and that it seemed more credible to quote a real fool than a figurative one. But if we look at the phrase in the light of the other quotations from Somer, it comes across quite simply as the words of a man who knows he is apt to put his foot in it, and who has been made aware of the fact, time and again. If it was he who was "nearly murdered" by Henry for slandering his mistress, then perhaps he had learned to be humble the hard way.

Since we can trace the saying to the last years of Henry's reign and one of his closest men, it is quite probable that it emanates from the intimate circle around the king. Both Paget's and Wotton's citations of the remark might be the trace of a private joke, an in-group reference that was comprehensible to only a small number of people. In itself, then, the utterance is unassuming, but its repetitions by illustrious men in Somer's own lifetime make it interesting as a glimpse of the humourous banter of the close circle around the king, where Somer certainly was a presence. In its original phrasing, it denotes the act of saying and promising more than one is able to keep, but also of saying things that might be fanciful or foolish. Read like that, it can be seen as a motto for any fool, but its context and origins close to the king, and the appendage of the words "as William Somer sayth," rather suggest that it became a motto for Somer specifically, and a characterisation of his manner of speaking. The coupling of this phrase with Nicholas Wotton's warm words about Somer in his letter—calling him a fellow and being unable to resist interposing an unrestrained wish for his well-being—further links the origin of the words with a close-knit courtly circle. Curiously, a passing mention of Somer in an anonymous Elizabethan pamphlet characterises him in a way that correlates with the impression we get. In a fictional dialogue between two elderly men, one of them expounds on the manner of speaking of various types of people—some rattle on, some speak hesitantly, some slowly, and so on. Then at the end of the list come those who "speake as if their words were made of wilde Hops: such mens tongues runne alwaies poasting before, and their wits come halting after; such a wit had *William Sommers*."[24]

The allusions to Somer in Paget's and Wotton's letters show Somer as the same bungler he is in Wilson's references. But in the context of the letters, they are probably mainly meant to convey a sense of familiarity with the court on a level that would have been possible for only a select few. We might draw the conclusion that Somer's fooling was accessible only to those close to the king, and therefore a sign of royal favour. In mentioning Somer they also use the fool as a reflection of themselves, but not in a way that is noticeably condescending. Wotton demonstrably establishes familiarity with Somer himself in a way that resembles affection for a close friend. There is even an undertone of concern for a man whose whereabouts seem to be unaccounted for. Judging from the documentation we have already reviewed, this seems unwarranted, as Queen Mary appears to have kept and clothed Somer in the same way as her predecessors on the throne. Or perhaps Wotton's words indicate an interlude in the beginning of Mary's reign where Somer was not at court, before he was once again taken up (maybe even after pressure from men like Wotton?). The details are unclear, but Wotton's tone is definitely a mixture of affection and concern, such emotions as one might have towards a friend who is unable to fend for himself. It is tempting to read Wotton's words as an attempt to emphasise his long-standing affiliation with the court. By expressing such intimacy with a man like Somer, who had by now been a court fool for over fifteen years, Wotton reminds his correspondent that he has been close to the throne for a long time. But Wotton and Petre were hardly rivals, as the intimate tone of their correspondence demonstrates. Both men rose to power around the same time in the late 1530s, and when Petre's health was failing in 1556, he wrote to Wotton to ask if he would succeed him as secretary of state. Consequently, there seems little reason to view Wotton's words as performative. The overall impression gained from his and Paget's references to Somer is one of affection for a man they seemed to like and with whom they congregated. Not on equal terms, but at least on a friendly basis.

Judging from our review of these brief and fragmented quotes of the court fool William Somer, then, what can we say about his role, his treatment, and his relationship to the surrounding court? The most manifest observation is perhaps how difficult it is to determine for certain his mental state. Apart from the first quotation about frauditors, conveyors, and deceivers, which he seems to have been coached, or coaxed, into saying, there is nothing here to suggest that Somer was a clever and deliberate comic. In a comparison of these instances of the fool's commentary with the documented remarks of other fools, Somer's distinctiveness emerges more clearly. Preserved utterances of natural fools are rare, but we are better served when considering those men about the court who combined the role of fool or jester with the role of writer or wit. One such man is the aforementioned John Heywood, who is recorded as uttering several wry comments in court circles. When placed alongside Somer's alleged words, these comments have a different character. When someone claimed that an increase in lawyers would undermine the profession, he is said to have replied: "No, for the more spaniels in the field the more game." This is a clear instance of symbolism and abstract thinking that is quite absent in what we have seen so far of Somer. When a man entertaining Heywood for dinner asked him whether he thought his beer was well hopped, Heywood replied: "It is very well hopped; but if it had hopped a little further, it had hopped into the water."[25] Here we see the use of a double meaning of a word similar to Somer's saying of the bishop's base voice, but in this form the underlying sarcasm is much more apparent. This could not be an unintentional mistake.

Another possible point of comparison is Somer's Jacobean successor in the role of the king's fool, Archie Armstrong. Armstrong was certainly a coarse and blustering fellow who is not easily placed in the natural or artificial category, but his documented sayings tell of a much more deliberate and forthright joker. While visiting Spain he was told about the infallibility of the pope, and that if the pope said a red coat was black, it was the truth. Armstrong retorted: "If the pope say soe, hee is ill of eyesight."[26] Armstrong's most famous comment was the one that caused him to be thrown out of court, when asking Archbishop Laud in his Scottish accent, "Whea's feale now?" after the disastrous attempt to impose the new book of common prayer in Scotland.[27] These constitute some of the more reliable quotations of Armstrong, and although they are not in the word-playing style of Heywood, they are much more intentional and satirical than Somer's. The remark about the pope could be an innocently expressed plain statement, but alongside the other comment, which is accompanied by several other documented instances wherein Armstrong used his position to point out the folly of others, it comes across as much more self-conscious. We see a more tangible notion of the fool that has surely evolved after Shakespearean drama and the consolidation of humanist interpretation. The age of Somer is more marked by fluid definitions and conceptions of what a fool ought to be.

We might further develop our picture of Somer's "wit" by considering one last anecdote with aspirations to authenticity. It is found in a book printed a few years after Somer's death, but it evidently originates from court gossip circulating in his own lifetime. It is related by Thomas Harding, a theologian and scholar who was at Oxford in the 1530s and '40s and achieved some status within the Protestant Church before explicitly embracing Catholicism, making him first a prominent priest during the reign of Mary, and then an exile in France after the accession of Elizabeth. It is in a book that seeks to refute the criticisms against the Catholic Church made by his colleague John Jewel that Harding mentions Somer. Listing the many "ifs" that he claims are the basis for Jewel's arguments, he warns of the danger of viewing these ifs as truths. "If all iffes were true," he begins, "then if heauen fell, we should catch larkes. And if a bridge were made betwen douer and Calys, we might go to Boleine a foote, as William Somer once tolde king Henry, if it be true that I haue heard saye."[28] This maxim is repeated in other books after this, but it seems to originate in Harding, who confesses to not having heard Somer say it himself, but thereby also confirms his connections with stories spread about the fool.[29] The reference to Boulogne certainly ties the saying to the time of the siege some years before, and it is similar to other quotes attributed to him, perhaps especially the words about the "base sermon," which is also a remark seemingly made in passing that betrays a predisposition to make unintentional solecisms. On one level it might be read as a type of rhetorical trick—the statement of the obvious to pierce the balloon of inflated oratory—and that is certainly how Harding uses it. But on another level it might just be something uttered by a natural fool in earnest and then utilised by someone else to make a point.

It cannot be said that Somer was considered a clever wit, but neither is there proof enough to cast him in the role of a disabled natural fool. His distinguishing characteristic is an inclination to make gaffes, to speak too quickly, the tongue that runs away while the wit comes halting after. Maybe he blabbered on, saying what came into his mind, now and then inadvertently stumbling upon a humourous phrasing or unwittingly saying something that could be imbued with comedy or betrayed a big mouth with an inadequately equivalent mind. He thus becomes a target for joking, a stooge or a flunky—unavoidably, given his title. A butt, surely, but not simply a target. A man viewed with affection and pity, like an impoverished uncle or a trusty old dog. Simultaneously a bully victim and a mascot, representing a fundamental social impulse that should be familiar to many school classes and army battalions, perhaps even workplaces.

William Somer is, in the eyes of the men quoted in this chapter, not a particularly noteworthy or important person.

But he is there, and whenever the topic moves into a certain area, he comes into view. In this way he is as invisible as a servant and useful to his surroundings only in certain regards—as an object of compassion and an unlearned voice whose utterances have the advantage of being empty and stupid enough to be filled with whatever humour and pregnancy the courtiers deem fit. He is a sort of distorting mirror who by his sheer folly allows the wit or thoughts of others to be twisted into something amusing and symbolic in its unintentional uncovering of a double meaning. The oft-mentioned practice of fools to "speak plainly" in front of their patrons says little about this situation. Somer could probably speak as plainly as he wanted, but he was so little regarded that it rarely seems to have gotten him into trouble. Therefore, he could be used both as a mouthpiece for someone with an axe to grind—like, perhaps, the person who Thomas Wilson thinks coached him into criticising Henry's accountants—and as a source of handy quotes for anyone who wanted a joke for a diatribe. It is possible to put this practice into a contemporary context by relating it to the Renaissance partiality for what one scholar has termed "involuntary *bon mots.*" The fool was considered the very emblem of this predilection, owing to the belief that he was himself unaware of the witty and cunning character of his own remarks. The humour and wisdom always relied on a third party who identified it. But the involuntary nature made the statement more valued than if it had been said knowingly by a clever comic.[30]

This relates to the conception of the fool as "man restored to his natural state," an aspect to which the contemporary courtier was highly ambivalent.[31] The people around Somer treasured his words and their spontaneous quality. Thomas

Wilson's suspicions concerning the true author of the joke about the accountants become quite natural in this context. It just seemed too premeditated. And yet, when other courtiers took up his words, they were infused with a new meaning. Somer's witticisms were thus always created through the combination of his own gaffes and the interpretations forced on them by those who spread them. Instilling his words with a deeper meaning was perhaps a way of making the fool's presence more respectable. Scepticism of fools was mainly reserved for their rowdiest qualities. This is also what to Wilson separates "common jesters" from clever wits.[32] Castiglione was similarly careful to distinguish between the courtier and the fool: "To make men laughe alwayes is not comelie for the Courtier, nor yet in suche wise as frantike, dronken, foolishe and fonde men and in like maner commune jesters do: and though to a mans thinkinge Courtes cannot be without suche kinde of persons, yet deserve they not the name of a Courtier."[33] Other writers also complained of the idle life of the courtier and of his inclination towards congregating with fools. Even Erasmus in his *Praise of Folly* offers a scathing description of the life of the courtier as frivolous and indolent, how they sleep till noon, play cards and dice, and mingle with "clowns, fools and whores."[34]

The rarity of allusions to Somer might be partly explained by the tension between the ideal of the courtier and the courtier's occasional fondness for fools. References to what the fool said or did were best kept to a minimum. This rhymes well with the picture gained in the previous chapter of the fool who is there but not regarded, sleeping in the background. It was wise to keep a healthy distance from the fool, so as not to be too much associated with him. John Heywood might have been thinking of Somer when he wrote the epigram entitled "Of choise to be a wise man or a foole." It sums up some of the points of *Witty and Witless*, but here the picture of the household fool is painted with an emphasis on his simultaneous presence and invisibility. Heywood's use of the seasons might also be a deliberate pun:

> Where best men in wynter syt next fyre from colde,
> There stāds the foole warme while all his tales be tolde.
> Which woldst thou be in sommer, when winter is gon?
> A foole. a foole, why? that why showth herevpon.
> In sommer when states syt from fyre in the coole,
> At that boordes end in coole ayre there stands the foole.
> Winter and sommer what tyme men must to wurke,
> Which woldst thou be? a foole to loke on and lurke.[35]

The epigram concludes that it is better to be a fool than a wise man, but this seems imbued with irony. The fool is warm in winter and cool in summer, thanks to his permitted presence in the halls of the mighty, but while wise men and men of rank sit down the fool stands. He is being looked at, and in a reiteration of John Bale's turn of phrase, he is "lurking." This is hardly an admired comic or extemporising clown on an elevated stage.

The fool stands in the corner, close to but excluded from the fellowship. The words are his, but their meaning others'. Present yet invisible, the courtiers refrain from looking straight at him, as a result of which his outline remains blurred to us.

CHAPTER 9

Role

HAVING COME this far, what do we know of William Somer?
There is some circumstantial evidence to support that he was
physically disciplined and roughly treated, at least in the beginning of his service. He took part in some Christmas festivals, playing the part of the Vice on at least one such occasion.
He may have been a collector of buttons. He became a sort of
symbol or mascot for the court and appeared in dynastic portraits as a mark of continuity from the reign of Henry VIII.
He was prone to drowsiness, or at least loitered about the
palaces languorously and lazily, like a cat or an old dog. But
he could also give in to violent outbursts, probably after being
provoked. There is at least one vague reference to Somer
being given to trembling, perhaps also stammering. The basis
of much of his alleged wit was the verbal gaffe, in which he
sometimes used a word the wrong way, and at times his jocu-
larity emanated from a tendency to make blunt or plain statements. Although not funny in themselves, these quips, in
combination with his humble status, became amusing for
being unexpected and inappropriate while not crossing the

line of decorum, because he was a fool. His alleged remark on friars and suggestion for a bridge across the channel are examples of this. Several references to his reluctance to "abide by" what he said indicate that this propensity for verbal slip-ups was a trademark and was well known among courtiers and to himself.

By all accounts, William Somer was an unassuming and uneducated man, with a willingness to rant that frequently revealed his lack of learning in relation to others at court. When he was a young fool, his status might have been less secure, and inappropriate remarks checked with physical punishment or rough forms of horseplay. But as the years went by, he seems to have found his place. He became a fixture of the royal palaces and, although still professing his verbal blunders, developed a knowledge of what would anger those around him and what would be appreciated. His discourse clearly amused and allowed his addressees the luxury of feeling both superior to this simpleminded man and an affinity (real or feigned) with the coarse and earthy nature of people outside the corridors of power.

Most likely, you had to be there. The writers who report his sayings seem to ride on a wave of appreciation of a private joke that cannot really be told out of context. In a closely knit circle—in this case, consisting only of men—the atmosphere easily becomes of such a sort that jokes do not require high-quality content for the laughter to come. Quite often it is a case of the sillier, the better. And maybe that is the factor that best describes and accounts for the court fool's quality and success—his participation in a private conversation, perhaps fuelled by alcohol, that turns increasingly frivolous and rowdy, requiring not so much a talent for comedy as an ability to maintain his own personality among men of a different background.[1] Then all he has to do is rely on the alcohol and the mutual egging on of the other participants to raise the mood of the party. And the morning after, everyone will recall that the fool said something that made them all roll about with laughter, but it is difficult to retell it out of context. The skill of the comedian that is easily forgotten, alongside an ability to make good jokes, is the ability to create an atmosphere in the audience that does part of the job for him.

If Somer had such a skill, or if he at least came to realise it, then he probably had a long way of getting there. The testimonies of his rough treatment and of his lashing out are vague, but they are found in several places. Although Somer's talent to amuse did not lie in a penchant for practical jokes, of which there is absolutely no contemporary documentation, his experience of being a fool was physical nonetheless. He cannot always have been meek and docile—the baiting environment of the court at its most frivolous and rowdy would have affected him and perhaps even exploited his bad temper or inability to fend for himself in an argument, quickly giving in to pointless hitting or shaking tantrums. Ascham's description of Somer striking innocent bystanders implies that there was another side to the chastisement of the fool. A man of sense and composure would never have dared to hit anyone at the court of Henry VIII, but Somer behaves as if he had nothing to lose. Perhaps he didn't.

Of William Somer outside the role of court fool we can say very little. There is a wardrobe account entry for a dress made for his sister when visiting him during the reign of Queen

Mary, and his burial record has him living in Shoreditch at the end of his life. But apart from that, his name is too common to connect the fool definitively to men with the same name in different records.[2] A letter of appeal to the Chancery Court around 1556 accuses two men named James Oswald and William Somer of stealing a horse from an old woman by purporting to confiscate it on a matter of royal business.[3] However, there is nothing to indicate that this Somer or James Oswald were connected to the court. In another case, a man named William Sommers claimed that he had been possessed by demons after offending a witch in 1598, an episode that was much publicised in pamphlets around the turn of the century.[4] It is frustrating to be left to pure speculation whenever we wish to examine Somer outside of the court context, and yet the paucity of records of him in any other guise or role might be revealing in itself. Any form of argument from silence is bound to be weak, of course, but at least it indicates quite clearly that Somer was a commoner—the type of person of which history is largely made up, and who barely leaves any mark in the record whatsoever.

Many aspects of the image we create of William Somer depend on how much we rely on Robert Armin's description of him. Although H. F. Lippincott was once very suspicious of Armin as a historian, recent scholars have been more positive. Sarah Carpenter treads a fine line between overreliance and overcriticism in an article on one of the other fools he described. "Armin is at pains to assert [his subjects'] historical actuality" by reporting place-names and patrons and by claiming his stories have been told by eyewitnesses, while at the same time Carpenter asserts that the "rhetorical form" of his book should keep the reader wary of its veracity.[5] Molly Clark takes a more cavalier stance in an article on the antecedents of the nonsense doggerel verse in *King Lear*. She traces its origins to "Will Sommers," basing her argument solely on the image of the rhyming games between Somer and the king drawn by Armin. Without interrogating the accuracy of this image, she claims that Somer "bequeathed" a "legacy of improvised rhyme" to "early modern culture."[6] If a tradition of improvised doggerel began in the sixteenth century, it did not originate with Somer. Richard Tarlton was probably guilty of popularising it, but he likely built on precursors such as John Skelton or the ribald flyting rhymes of Scottish poets such as William Dunbar and David Lindsay.[7]

In this account, I have steered clear of Armin's picture of Somer as much as possible, mainly because many of Somer's characteristics in Armin's portrayal are difficult to square with the image that has emerged through a consideration of the primary sources. A sceptical stance towards Armin has also allowed us to create a picture of Somer and his role without being coloured by Armin's posthumous perspective. Armin's version of Somer is undoubtedly more domesticated than he has come across here, and it is possible that the aggressive sides he attributes to other fools originally came from Somer. But a few of the details in his account might be extracted to elaborate the sketchy portrait I have painted. Apart from the story of his sleepiness, supported by Heywood's words, there is the story of his poor uncle's visit to court. But most appealing is the passing remark that after his rhyming game with the king, he laid himself "downe amongst the Spaniels to sleep." This is an image so outré and conspicuous that it is difficult not to wonder whether it is founded in truth. If not, then it reflects in a curious way the notion we have acquired of Somer's place and character—inherently humble and domesticated, falling asleep as easily on a gate as in a dog's basket.

All things considered, the man at the centre of this book does not appear to have done much intentionally to be where he was, or to become who he became. He did not end up as Henry VIII's fool by pure accident, of course, but I hesitate to consider it a consequence of his own determined agency. The impression of passivity might in itself have been intentional, in which case he becomes a highly skilled master of appearing to do nothing in order to be funny, but that feels too much like a roundabout interpretation and a bit of wishful thinking. The things that Somer did and said that stand out are interesting to dwell on—like his incessant falling asleep or his garbling of words—and they come together to draw a picture of a man who was given much leeway to do and say what he liked. But by this we should not talk in terms of the legendary "fool's licence," the notion that fools were permitted to criticise authority and their employers because they were fools. If Somer was the fool who was nearly murdered for insulting the queen and princess in 1535, then he certainly lived to regret it. The fool rather comes across as a person who perpetually lived in a sort of parallel dimension to the other people at court, whose very way of life was meant to be an antithesis to the diligence of servants or the rationality and responsibility of politicians and kings. In Somer we do not see the excessive drinking that we see in many other fools—from Patch to the eighteenth-century dwarf Perkeo, known for being able to hold enormous amounts of wine and whose nickname derives from the Italian for "Why not?"—a clear sign of the carnivalesque spirit that was meant to permanently surround the fool. But his detachment from all other areas of court business, including other forms of entertainment, certainly indicates a type of isolation.

From what we can tell, Somer was permitted to go about the court in this parallel existence so that he might provide fodder for amusement to others and stir humour and contemplation in those around him. A sort of human conversation piece, if you like. In the way that Thomas Wilson took up Somer's clumsy remark about a bishop's base voice, courtiers could observe the fool and use his doings and sayings as a source for their own musings. It has become common among historians of fools to portray them as prototypes of the entertainers that would emerge closer to the modern age, standing in front of an audience and making jokes to the enjoyment of all. But when examining Tudor fools up close, it is difficult to see any real continuity between them and the Elizabethan clowns. Although these later stage performers were also referred to as "fools"—especially by themselves—they initiated a formative type of stage comedy with more direct links to subsequent centuries than its predecessors. Together with the zanies of the emerging commedia dell'arte of continental theatre, these were the first truly professional stage comics. But what did this new form of comic owe to the Renaissance court fool? When we focus on the pre-Shakespearean age of William Somer and his colleagues, there is very little to suggest that fools were performers in front of an audience.

We might take as a point of comparison Thomas More's household fool Henry Patenson. Very little is known about Patenson, but a description of him in Thomas Stapleton's 1588 biography of More has been used to create a picture of a popular entertainer who amused the More family after dinner. What Stapleton actually says, however, is merely that after the serious dinner conversation, More "would suggest some light topic, and all would be highly amused. Henry Patenson, More's fool, would now join in the conversation."[8] The source of amusement, then, is not Patenson. It is only stated that the conversation was of such a type that he could take part in it. In the only study devoted to Patenson, Noeline Hall refers to him as "a fool in the medieval tradition, employed to provide pure fun."[9] This image is arrived at somewhat haphazardly, however, and an examination of the available evidence gives a more complex picture. Hall also mentions an anecdote about Patenson told by Ellis Heywood in his celebratory dialogue on Thomas More from 1556. Here Patenson is credited with a joke about the size of a guest's nose at a feast. When chided for his remark, he overcompensates and says that the man in fact has no nose at all. Heywood concludes by noting that "everybody laughed so hard . . . they almost dislocated their jaws."[10] But this anecdote is stolen from Heywood's father, our old friend John Heywood, whose epigram "Of the foole and the gentlemans nose" relates the same story.[11] Here, however, it is not attributed to Patenson, and, as Mark Robson has pointed out, it does not end with riotous laughter. On the contrary, Heywood père's fool is rebuked. The congregation is provoked and angered by his remarks, and he is eventually beaten for his transgression.[12]

Although Heywood's tale is not related to Patenson, it further elucidates how the image of the fool as a comic table-side entertainer emerges only when the fool is fictionalised. No reliable primary sources of the sixteenth century contain a concrete depiction of any fool behaving in this way. The accounts of Somer's words that we examined in the last chapter indicate that the fool entertained by making utterances that people found amusing, but this appears to have been done in conversation with a group of people, who might have teased out simpleminded or naive comments to report to their acquaintances. There is no sign of any conscious jest or deliberate performance. The remark about the big nose in the Heywoods' works is not made in a performance. John Heywood states that the fool in his version of the tale was "standyng by," and Ellis Heywood likewise describes him as "standing by my table while we were eating." The entertainment provided by the fool was thus not an item on the programme separate from the other events of a feast, but integrated into the sociability and interaction of the others present. Like Patenson, he joined in the conversation. The fool was not spatially removed onto a stage or anything similar, but stood by—close but hardly equal.

Only in Ellis Heywood's amended version are the fool's words immediately taken as humourous. The fool in John Heywood's version appears to be kept just as much to provoke anger. Of those Tudor fools about whom we might tease out some reliable information, there are a few whose attraction appears to have been based on anger or frustration. John Pace, who was first fool to the Duke of Norfolk and then at the court of Elizabeth, was referred to posthumously as "Pace the bitter fool." Francis Bacon claims that when the queen said, "Come on, Pace; now we shall hear of our faults," he replied, "I do not use to talk of that that all the town talks of."[13] Another fool at Elizabeth's court, an Italian known as Monarcho, appears to have been a delusional megalomaniac who considered himself a great monarch and became easily embroiled in disputes with people in his surroundings concerning this. His self-importance and arrogance were what others found funny in him, and laid the basis for his engagement as royal fool, but judging from the many contemporary references to him, and a brief epitaph by Thomas Churchyard, he was unaware of how others perceived him. Churchyard speaks of his "taunting tongue," which was "pleasant sharp."[14]

These fools reflect the conditions of court foolery at Somer's time, showing how fools were not performers but butts and how the humour derived from the fool's clashes with those around him, oftentimes the undoubtedly mocking laughter at a person who is angry and frustrated for being misunderstood—and perhaps for never being taken seriously.[15] But simply identifying these fools as bully victims and butts of jokes does little to explain their positions or the context of foolery practice. What to a modern viewer comes across as bullying and mocking had a meaning in itself to the sixteenth-century courtier. In his instructions to courtiers, Castiglione famously advocated what he called *sprezzatura*, a type of wit that evades affectation and conveys effortlessness and natural grace. When inciting this manner, he also, as we have touched on, stresses the need for distance between the courtier and the fool and encourages sophisticated displays of wit in duels of repartee in favour of taunting and mockery; but paradoxically, the emphasis on the natural in Castiglione's ideal also feeds into the culture of the court fool.

"We may call that art true art which does not seem to be art," Castiglione says.[16] Looking at the practice of fools and the attitudes toward fools in the situational rather than the philosophical, we see how fools were cherished for their artlessness and lack of affectation. In Somer especially, it is clear that the fool illustrates a wish for authenticity in the courtly circles, or for a reminder of authenticity within the performative context of the court.[17] To what extent this down-to-earth-ness was authentic we cannot safely say, but in some cases the traits that qualified a person as a natural fool might have exempted them from the inherent performativity of court society, to which I alluded in chapter 3. The aspect of authenticity makes it somewhat reductive to interpret the appraisal of the spontaneous and naive nature of the fool as mockery or condescension. That such interpretations do not quite hit the mark becomes apparent when we see that the qualities of the fool were not only, or perhaps not even chiefly, treasured as a source of comedy. According to Indira Ghose, humour was still very much seen as an antidote to melancholy, in line with the thinkers of antiquity, and not until the end of the sixteenth century and the great Elizabethan transformation of the theatre were laughter and comedy popularised and made into a form of entertainment rather than a remedy.[18] To what extent this applies to popular culture and everyday humour is open to question, of course, but it serves to move our conception of humour away from the modern outlook. To view the Renaissance fool as a precursor to the modern comedian, then, is in some ways a misunderstanding, even if the legacy of fools often came to emphasise the humourous aspects of them, or even turned them into skillful proto-clowns.

Castiglione's edicts came about in an age when laughter was very much associated with aggressiveness and jeering and should probably be read as a reaction against the vulgar humour that he saw as seeping into the court circles—a reaction famously interpreted by Elias as a sign of the court's need to distinguish itself in an increasingly complex and socially mobile society.[19] We could attempt a conclusion based on the fact that the few allusions to physical chastisement of Somer come only from early in his career, while later references concern his conversation or participation in court ceremony. Was the fool also a part of the attempt to "civilise" the court and abolish the type of rowdy humour among courtiers that Castiglione condemned—pushing each other down stairs, causing each other's horses to roll over, or throwing soup and gravy in people's faces at dinner?[20] There is not enough evidence to identify a clear change during the century, although the attitude toward and role of Somer do stand out as more complex in relation to previous fools, and there are no records of successors such as Archie Armstrong or Jeffrey Hudson being beaten.

Most histories of the fool see its origins in the combined trajectories of such medieval occupations as minstrels, jugglers, and players, but the very special nature of the "entertainment" and function of the Renaissance fool sets him apart from these other groups, in the same way that Will Somer is never grouped together with them in contemporary records. So maybe we should look for the precursors to stage clowns in these other categories. The fool, on closer inspection, appears to be something quite different. In the sixteenth century, and perhaps especially in the courts of northern Europe, the fool was still an expression of medieval theological and ritual considerations rather than an entertainer. At the Henrician court, he might have started to turn into a concession to Erasmian humanism, but in the guise of William Somer was still very much a threshold character, symbolising a transition from scapegoat to remedy for melancholy. By the seventeenth century, the role and treatment of the court fool had certainly changed, not exactly from violence to respect, but from spontaneity and unpredictability to ceremonial and organisation. Peter Happé credits Erasmus with popularising the idea of the fool's wisdom and holiness, and it is clear that the sixteenth century constituted a transition in the attitude toward the fool in northern Europe, especially England (a transition that might already have occurred in Italy and France).[21] The appointment and persistence of William Somer can be seen as an expression of a conscious ambition in Henry to keep a new type of fool, perhaps even as a deliberate part of his distancing from Rome and adoption of the ideas of new thinkers like Erasmus. Virtually all leaders at this time kept a fool, including the pope, but there are some indications that the fools of some potentates, including the pope, were of a more boisterous and bullied type.[22] Somer's career might illustrate a turning point in the role of English court fools, from a beaten butt of jokes to a beloved retainer—a mascot.

Although Somer's recorded sayings are exciting in themselves, it is perhaps in the records of his actions and behaviour that we get even closer to him. In the anecdotes, we glimpse a stranger trying to keep up with the conversation of men from a different social and cultural sphere. A complete fool in the strange environment in which he found himself, but perhaps like any other had he stayed in his hometown or village.[23] The simultaneous amusement and affection awakened in people around him are to a great extent the same reactions that a simpleminded or spontaneous individual arouses in one's surroundings even today. It is the foundation for many popular media personalities and celebrities, some of whom have attained their status for being laughed at and not quite understanding why.

But was there such a vast difference between the speech and thinking of courtiers and that of rural commoners in the sixteenth century as to explain the appeal of fools? Many historians have recently emphasised the mutual influence and close relations between oral and literate cultures in early modern England, and several aspects of popular culture existed across the social spectrum.[24] But there were also, of course, social and geographic divisions, and historians of speech, including particularly Peter Burke, have noted how there were many ways in which early modern people discerned between elite and commoner—accent, vocabulary, polite phrases, and so on.[25] More importantly, however, the world of the courtier and gentry in the sixteenth century and onwards was preoccupied with what has been termed self-fashioning and the formation of identities that separated them from their inferiors, or from anyone of a different social sphere.[26] We have seen how the fool could become a tool in such efforts, a sort of countertype against which a person of the court might contrast themself.[27]

The fool was not just a distorting mirror but also a mirror image that flattered whoever was looking at it.[28]

As asserted by Anu Korhonen, the fool was humourous "through the definitions and interpretations others applied in observing him."[29] The comedy did not derive from what the fool did as much as from what others did to the fool. We have seen here signs that the fool was viewed as a generator of humour rather than a bearer of humour—an empty vessel to be filled by observers with interpretations of the strange things he said. In his tendency to utter "involuntary *bon mots*," they appealed to the comic taste of the Renaissance. But by moving closer to the day-to-day treatment and practice of the fool, we glimpse the difficulty of keeping socially distanced or uneducated, to say nothing of disabled, commoners at court. Korhonen and Sarah Carpenter explained the coexistence of affection and aggression in the attitude toward the fool with the simultaneous grace and sinfulness of the fool in theology. But might there not also be a more practical explanation? Courtiers and kings knew that it was fashionable and advisable to keep a fool, and they enjoyed their company to be sure, but the discrepant roles and lack of understanding of the fool's lot must also quite naturally have resulted in clashes. Once again, the parallel of the pet comes to mind.

In our close study of William Somer, we have seen several roles that the court fool could fill in the sixteenth century: a good-luck charm, a human conversation piece, a symbol of authenticity, and a generator of humour in his interactions with others rather than a self-contained vessel of humour. The fool as a mascot or charm is perhaps the function that has been the most recurrent in our observations of Somer.

This function encompasses not just his continuous and necessary presence, whose obscure justification so baffled John Heywood, but also his emerging role as a symbol of Tudor continuity and as a reminder of the world outside to the noble courtiers.

The extant documentation makes it easy to form an impression of the fool as only a passive agent made into a source of laughter or a symbol of something only by others. The court, in a way, shaped Will Somer the fool. But how did Somer shape the court? To answer this question, we must be even more speculative. Based on what we have observed, we must also consider the contexts that we know but which do not show themselves in the sources on Somer. Perhaps the most blatant absence in these records is the relationship between Somer and the monarchs he served. During Henry's reign, he was at least "the king's fool," and so he must have attended him in his private chambers, being present on numerous occasions. Henry VIII's closest man on a purely geographic level, perhaps, but apparently seldom regarded. An invisible man, if ever there was one. If he engaged in rhyming battles with the king, then it is quite a stretch to believe that the very neat verses recorded by Armin were the same ones improvised in the king's chamber. This would require the verses to be orally transmitted from those present (according to Armin, only Somer and the king) to others at court, and someone who either wrote them down or memorised them for a very long time. No, no, that is certainly not the Will Somer we have pieced together here.

If he had an impact on the court and the king, it was one of showing them occasional glimpses of a person who did not behave as they did or according to courtly customs, who spoke like a man from the world outside, and who gave them momentary tastes of vernacular speech and unlettered lines of reasoning. Most times this would have made them laugh or sneer, but his endurance and behaviour also aroused their sympathy and affection. Maybe it was a test of character for new courtiers, to see whether their affected manners could hold up to the down-to-earth-ness of Will Somer. For the longer-serving men at court, a show of affinity with Somer was a sign of their maturity—their identity was not threatened by the presence of this man from the world outside. In this process, they presumably also learned something. If he had not been there, would not the court have lost a dimension of humanity? Was he not there to show these men of power, who casually started wars and diplomatic crises, that there were other men, men whose lives were affected by their haphazard decisions? If he was, it was largely in vain, unless he did imbue some with a tinge of compassion or hesitation.

But the fool stands as a symbol of something fundamental to history—the simple individual in the midst of great events, an unavoidable victim, vainly trying to show the panjandrums the ordinary people at the receiving end of their choices. And to walk among them as a mirror showing them that they are the same, if only one of them had stopped to look. Thither he lingers awhile, irrespective of whether he is regarded, before quietly lumbering out of the lamplight to sleep with the spaniels.

CHAPTER 10

Legacy

THE MODERN comedian is a revered artist. Scholars and critics nowadays pour over the works of Chaplin, Pryor, and Hope just as much as the works of poets and painters. It was not always like that, however. We need only go back a few decades to see the traces of a suspicion towards humour as a serious object of study, and before the modern-age clowns and fools were at the absolute bottom of the social scale. Occasionally we get glimpses of how it might have been, like when an enraged audience member walks onstage and slaps a stand-up comedian, or when a ruler orders the killing of a satirist who has mocked him. Some things are eternal, like the ease with which a comic mocks a tyrant, or the equal ease with which the tyrant hangs the comic for mocking him. The rage and fury unleashed by such clashes between tyranny and derision reveal how the history of comic entertainers is not only, or even mainly, about humour.

When writers casually claim that the modern comedian derives from the Renaissance fool, it is an appealing thought, and there are certainly descriptions of Elizabethan clowns and railers that could just as easily be about twenty-first-century stand-up comedians. In one of his early films, Woody Allen plays a medieval court fool who performs before his employer just like a late twentieth-century comic ("That plague is really something, isn't it?").[1] In the previous chapter, I questioned the role of the court fool as a stage performer and entertainer, but I would assert that the link between the fool and the comedian is there, only more complex than it appears at first glance. In this brief coda, I will situate the subject of this book in the history of comedy by considering the legacy that William Somer left behind. It is a legacy that still influences comedy, but which rather than being achieved by him, was, as it were, thrust upon him.

Much ink has been spilled on Hamlet's criticism of clowns in his advice to the actors. This makes me hesitate to allude to it, but at least one line in that speech is an illuminative illustration of the role William Somer and men of his ilk have played in the history of comedy. Hamlet dismisses clowns that improvise beyond the script, tell the same jokes every time, and make faces to elicit laughter. But he also remarks that there are some clowns that "will laugh themselves, to set on some quantity of barren spectators to laugh with them." This, in Hamlet's mind, is vile and shows a "pitiful ambition in the fool that useth it."[2]

Hamlet's words can be read as indicating a dislike of clowns, or fools—the words are here used interchangeably—who try too hard to make the audience laugh. By extension, it can also be read as an aversion to fools who laugh at their own jokes and who know that they are funny, or, in other words, artificial fools. This attitude toward comedians can be found today as well, either in the antipathy towards stand-up comedians whose efforts to make audiences like them or laugh are too obvious, or in the preference for "deadpan comedy" as opposed to broad humour or hamming.[3] What Shakespeare vents here is a distinction that was to become fundamental in modern comedy—the difference between a highbrow preference for subdued and subtle comedy, on the one hand, and a lowbrow preference for loud and vulgar comedy, on the other. To what extent this distinction is consistent, and how it relates to social or cultural dimensions is debatable, but one does not need to study modern comedy for long to encounter it and be certain it exists in the minds of many. The writers of the Elizabethan period—and above all Shakespeare—wished to demonstrate their distance from earlier low forms of comedy, both in their development of comedic style and in their outright condemnation of broad comedy, as in Hamlet's speech.

The gist of Hamlet's words is the self-consciousness of the fool, which he does not like. When *Hamlet* was first performed, Shakespeare had begun a working relationship with the clown Robert Armin, for whom he would write some of his most famous clown roles, including Touchstone in *As You Like It*, Feste in *Twelfth Night*, and the Fool in *King Lear*. Armin's well-documented interest in historical fools in general, and natural fools in particular, has been seen as a great influence on these characterisations and on the fact that Shakespeare's clowns, which earlier were rustic simpletons or servants, now become household or court fools. The dim-witted servants of the earlier comedies, like Lancelot Gobbo in *The*

Merchant of Venice or Lance in *The Two Gentlemen of Verona*, while not exactly self-conscious fools, are tricksters and carousers, playing more to the audience than being part of the fiction of the play. The later clowns exist in that middle ground between natural and artificial fool which Armin explores in *Foole upon Foole*, and their wit is clever, but they never give in to the hamming of the earlier clowns, and they always deliver their witty lines in a wry, subtle manner. Needless to say, these later clowns are much easier for modern actors to play, whereas it seems more demanding to be funny when playing Lancelot Gobbo or Peter in *Romeo and Juliet*—roles that are often abridged or cut when the plays are performed.

So Shakespeare, in a way, was an early proponent of deadpan comedy. His suspicion of loud clowns came from experience, one might presume, and this was possibly the case for his fondness for subdued fools as well, though this was most likely nourished by Robert Armin's influence. In fact, all three fools played by Armin that I mentioned above—Touchstone, Feste, and Lear's fool—have been connected to William Somer by various writers.[4] In every case, however, this is done quite haphazardly, and one could just as well conclude that Armin's fool roles are based on a generic fool character. But as we saw in chapter 2, the name Will Somer, or "Will Sommers," was by this time synonymous with court fools. A different affinity between Hamlet's words and William Somer is the preference for fools who do not laugh at themselves and who are, as it were, indeliberately funny. Preferring a comedian who does not laugh at their own jokes to one who laughs helplessly after each punchline is quite obvious in contemporary culture. Likewise, we often find it funnier when comic protagonists fall over without joining in the laughter afterwards, or when comedians are unaware of their own silliness or misfortune. One cannot deny that there is a brutal aspect of comedy, and I would not be the first to ask what this has to do with laughing at other people's misfortunes and with finding humour in people with disabilities in the early modern age.

As this study has shown, a defining quality of the humour of fools was its spontaneous and inadvertent nature. As noted by Metzler, there was presumably a market for fools who emulated the behaviour of the natural, and if they were never found out, they could have a successful career. One example is Cacurgus, the fool of the play *Misogonus*, who plays the part of a natural but who is actually shrewd and scheming. The fact that he is so often referred to as "Will Summer" suggests that a common belief at the time held Somer to be exactly the type of fake that many suspected fools of being. The fear of fakes reveals the nature of kept fools and their cherished qualities.[5] If the fool showed any sign of understanding his own misfortune or stupidity, it was all ruined. Behind all this was a suspicion surrounding any comedy that was contrived or artificial. Famously, Sir Philip Sidney agreed with Hamlet in criticising the theatrical clown vogue, since the aim of clowns was not to "imitate humanity."[6] The gist of this critique is most often taken to be the scepticism of clowns in plays other than comedies, but there is also here a sense that clowns come in the way of an attempt at a more refined type of comedy.

Although the words "clown" and "fool" could be used synonymously towards the end of the sixteenth century, when theatrical clowns were an established phenomenon, they denoted different types of persons whose common denominator was considered to be stupidity. The clown was a rustic, boor, or peasant, often attributed with rude ways and simplemindedness. The word "fool" denoted what today would be described as a person with a learning or intellectual disability. Thus, for instance, in John Florio's 1598 Italian-English dictionary, in the explanations of Italian words for "peasant," he often couples words such as "rustic," "countryman," "ploughman," "boor," and "gross fellow" with the word "clown." "Fool" is coupled with "ninny," "sot," "dolt," "gull," "idiot," or "patch." In a few entries, "fool" and "clown" are used together, especially in words appertaining to stage characters.[7] In many books of the late sixteenth century, "fool" and "clown" are used together to describe roughly the same things, but mostly they are listed separately as two different types of dullards. For example, in his admonition against the theatre, William Rankins enumerates separate character types when speaking of actors: "some trans-formed themselues to Roges, other to Ruffians, some other to Clownes, a fourth to fooles, in the fift place Louers and Leachers."[8] In *Wit, Fits and Fancies*, Anthony Copley devotes separate chapters to fools and "countrymen and clowns."[9]

But did this mean that the fool was preferred to the clown when it came to laughing at them? We see above all in the example of Armin and Shakespeare's collaboration how they tried to absorb the tradition of the natural household fool into the creation of a new type of clown character molded on the old fools of folklore. It has been suggested that

Armin wrote *Foole upon Foole* as a sort of poetics for his own "new kind of fool" that would emerge from this conglomerate.[10] Contrary to what has often been claimed, then, Armin's roles in Shakespeare did not constitute a move from the natural fools of earlier comedy to artificial fools.[11] The distinction between these two types was more complex than it seems, as this book in some ways has shown. This is related to the lack of interest from Thomas Wilson and others regarding whether Somer was a natural fool. In his fool characterisations, Armin assimilated what he saw as the inherent wisdom of the natural fools, resulting in the clever fool characters that he originated—Feste, Touchstone, Lavatch, and so forth. Both Armin and Shakespeare, then, saw more wisdom in natural fools than in face-pulling clowns who became a hallmark of what we would call lowbrow comedy. Hence the difficulty for modern critics of deciding whether King Lear's fool is a natural or artificial fool.[12] And Shakespeare's new fools have been seen as representative of an increasing dismissal of the earlier type of clowns, as well as an attempted banishment of clowns from theatre altogether.[13] As Shakespeare succinctly put it in one of his plays: "Sweet clown, sweeter fool."[14]

When we enter the seventeenth-century era of Puritanism and civil war, the conditions for foolery and clowning are fundamentally different. The clown never fully died, resurfacing in marginal forms during the Interregnum (mainly through Robert Cox, who illegally performed garbled Shakespeare farces[15]) and the Restoration, but he certainly changed appearances. The fool lived on as well, but now in the reincarnation of the court jester, the still very bawdy and coarse but also skilled and urbane comedian whose connections to the fools of the previous century were mainly in the form of nostalgic evocation and claiming of a continuous tradition. Provincial household fools like Tom Skelton, fool to the Earl of Crawford, or Black John of Tetcott—who swallowed mice tied to a string, then pulled them back up again—might have been creatures of the Tudor era as much as of the late seventeenth and early eighteenth centuries.[16] Enlightenment historian Dorina Outram has shown how court fools in the German states could be particularly raucous and vulgar well into the eighteenth century, but this type of fool was a dying breed, surviving only in some parts of Europe. At most courts, the vogue was for dwarfs—in England the renowned Jeffrey Hudson and then Conrad Kopperman, the last official dwarf of the royal household—or "court moors," Black people from the West Indies or Africa.[17] Dwarfs and moors could entertain or participate in court revels, but primarily they functioned as servants or royal officials. The contrasting role that fools and dwarfs had had was slowly succeeded by an ideology of civilising colonialism.[18]

But the impact of the Renaissance natural fool lived on in an enduring predilection for the indeliberate aspect of true humour. Can we say that Will Somer himself played a role in popularising this type of comedy? As we saw in the previous chapter, he did not become a legend of foolery by his own choice, but when studying him, we cannot ignore the role that his posthumous reputation might have played in the development of comedy from the end of the sixteenth century onwards. Somewhere in the posthumous mythologisation of

Somer, and the commingling of his figure with those of Richard Tarlton and earlier mythical fools such as Scoggin, one might unearth a backstory for the comedy that truly came to light in the Elizabethan period, probably through an expansion of print and theatre. When the theatres grew in quantity and popularity, and pamphlet "hacks" became increasingly greedy and sensational, discerning critics quickly grew weary of exactly the type of humour and clowning derided by Hamlet. The prototypical comic figure was the fool, who by definition did not know that he was funny. And even though Shakespeare and Armin changed the appearance of the fool, the basis was still the same.

And it is still the same: the man (it is still mostly a man) who does not see or understand his own misfortune or stupidity.[19] Early modern laughter at natural fools was about authenticity and superiority, and the knowledge that the person found funny was funny by accident or unaware of the source for comedy. The fool is, in some way, the perfect comedian. In the same way that a person living life while being secretly filmed would be the perfect actor. If we could, we would perhaps like to have completely unsuspecting people being subjected to humiliation and obstacles as our entertainment. Our ethics prevent us from doing so, unless one counts reality television. Enid Welsford concluded that the attraction of the fool lay in the fact that the taunting of him never transcended into mere bullying. Because the fool is "none the worse for his slapping," the abuses he is subjected to become therapeutic rather than offensive.[20] But the question is, Does this apply a modern sensibility on a premodern culture that is more vicious than we like to think? In the words of Mel Brooks, "Tragedy is when I cut my finger. Comedy is when you fall into an open sewer and die."[21]

This premodern culture is still there under the surface, and yet I am reluctant to characterise the fool as simply an early modern equivalent of the comedian. He was laughed at, sometimes, and certainly paved the way for the later emergence of clowns and comics, but he was himself not primarily a comedian. Or if he was, it was purely by accident.

Notes

Abbreviations

BL   British Library

LMA   London Metropolitan Archives

NA   National Archives

Chapter One

1. Alison Weir, *Henry VIII: King & Court* (London: Vintage, 2008), 251. The scene appears to be taken from the 1637 jest biography about Somer, but there is no reference. Tracy Borman reproduces Weir's scene in her own book *Henry VIII and the Men Who Made Him* (London: Hodder, 2019), 250.

2. A step towards a reappraisal of the subject of the fool was taken in a Wellcome Trust–funded project entitled "All the King's Fools," led by Suzannah Lipscomb in 2011, in which Tudor fools were studied as people with learning disabilities. The main outcome of the project was a performance project at Hampton Court Palace. The research was presented to the public only in the form of a brief popular article and a talk by Lipscomb at Hampton Court. Cf. Suzannah Lipscomb, "All the King's Fools," *History Today*, 61: 8 (2011), 6–7; and Suzannah Lipscomb, "Playing the Fool," lecture at Hampton Court Palace, May 2017. Lipscomb has, however, kindly shared her notes with me.

3. The primary modern overviews of the history of the fool include Enid Welsford, *The Fool: His Social and Literary History* (London: Faber & Faber, 1935); William Willeford, *The Fool and His Sceptre: A Study in Clowns and Jesters and Their Audience* (Evanston, IL: Northwestern University Press, 1969); Sandra Billington, *A Social History of the Fool* (Brighton, UK: St. Martin's Press, 1984); John

Southworth, *Fools and Jesters at the English Court* (Stroud, UK: Sutton, 1998); Beatrice K. Otto, *Fools Are Everywhere: Court Jesters around the World* (Chicago: University of Chicago Press, 2001). Welsford's book has been formative, and although it relies on earlier anecdotal histories, it contains important observations. The most serious scholarly work is found in Billington and Southworth, although both are occasionally haphazard and erroneous. The extensive book by Otto is entertaining and far-reaching but unfortunately too impressionistic to be relied on as a standard work. Cf. Sandra Billington's scathing review of it in *Folklore*, 113: 1 (2002), 111–12. For a concise survey of the historiography on fools, cf. Dorinda Outram, *Four Fools in the Age of Reason: Laughter, Cruelty, and Power in Early Modern Germany* (Charlottesville: University of Virginia Press, 2019).

4. On Zúñiga, see George Mariscal, "A Clown at Court: Francesillo de Zuñiga's *Crónica burlesca*," in *Autobiography in Early Modern Spain*, ed. by Nicholas Spadaccini & Jenaro Talens (Minneapolis, MN: Prisma Institute, 1988), 59–76. The preserved diaries of two jesters at the court of Urbino in the sixteenth century were written by men of aristocratic origins and say very little about the life and outlook of fools. Cf. Tito Saffioti, *'E il signor duca ne rise di buona maniera': Vita privata di un buffone di corte nella Urbino del Cinquecento* (Milan: La Vita Felice, 1997); Alessandro Gnocchi, "'Quel bastardo del Dio d'amor': Il diario del buffone Giovannaccio (1561)," *Anticomoderno*, 5 (2001), 73–104.

5. The few pieces of writing attributable to early modern clowns deliberately mock learning. Cf. Will Kemp, *Kemps nine daies wonder. Performed in a daunce from London to Norwich* (London: Nicholas Ling, 1600); Tristano Martinelli, *Compositions de Rhétorique de Monsieur Don Arlequin* (Lyon, 1601); Hugh Roberts, "Medicine and Nonsense in French Renaissance Mock Prescriptions," *Sixteenth Century Journal*, 40: 3 (2009), 721–44.

6. Thomas Nashe, *The Unfortunate Traveller and Other Works*, ed. by J. B. Steane (London: Penguin Books, 1972), 192.

7. Janet L. Nelson, "Writing Early Medieval Biography," *History Workshop Journal*, 50: 1 (2000), 129–36 (130–31).

8. Natalie Zemon Davis, *Trickster Travels: A Sixteenth-Century Muslim between Worlds* (New York: Hill & Wang, 2006).

9. Maxine Berg, "Crossing Boundaries," *History Workshop Journal*, 65 (2008), 227–33 (231).

10. Natalie Zemon Davis, *The Return of Martin Guerre* (Cambridge, MA: Harvard University Press, 1983), viii.

11. Hannu Salmi, "Cultural History, the Possible and the Principle of Plenitude," *History & Theory*, 50: 2 (2011), 171–87 (187).

12. Eva Österberg, "De tystas biografi," in *På cykeltur genom livet: En vänbok till Gunnar Wetterberg*, ed. by Sven E. O. Hort (Stockholm: Atlantis, 2013), 20. The translation is my own.

13. This is especially applicable to the books by Willeford, Billington, and Otto.

14. Cf. Phebe Jensen's review of it in *Early Theatre*, 4 (2001), 185–87.

15. Disability studies and disability history have evolved rapidly over the past thirty or so years. For concise overviews of the theoretical development of disability history, from the constructivist approach of Rosemarie Garland-Thomson to the emphasis on an interaction between social, medical, and cultural factors in the works of Metzler, Goodey, McDonagh, and others, cf. Alice Equestri, *Literature and Intellectual Disability in Early Modern England: Folly, Law and Medicine, 1500-1640* (New York: Routledge, 2022), 11–14; and Susan Anderson & Liam Haydon, "Introduction," in *A Cultural History of Disability in the Renaissance*, ed. by Susan Anderson & Liam Haydon (London: Bloomsbury, 2020), 10–11. The book that pioneered early modern disability studies is *Recovering Disability in Early Modern England*, ed. by Allison P. Hobgood & David Houston Wood (Columbus: Ohio State University Press, 2013). The main works studying early modern disability from a sociohistorical perspective are C. F. Goodey, *A History of Intelligence and "Intellectual Disability": The Shaping of Psychology in Early Modern Europe* (London: Routledge, 2011); Irina Metzler, *Fools and Idiots? Intellectual Disability in the Middle Ages* (Manchester: Manchester University Press, 2016); *Intellectual Disability: A Conceptual History, 1200-1900*, ed. by Patrick McDonagh, C. F. Goodey, & Tim Stainton (Manchester: Manchester University Press, 2018).

16. Equestri, *Literature and Intellectual Disability*, 129, 215.

17. Wes Folkerth, "Reading Shakespeare after Neurodiversity," in *Performing Disability in Early Modern English Drama*, ed. by Leslie C. Dunn (Cham: Springer, 2020), 141–57.

18. J. R. Mulryne, "Somer, William," in *Oxford Dictionary of National Biography*, ed. by H. C. G. Matthew & Brian Harrison (Oxford: Oxford University Press, 2004) (hereafter *ODNB*).

19. Metzler, *Fools and Idiots*, 196.

20. Nashe, *Unfortunate Traveller*, 147 (my emphasis).

Chapter Two

1. 'S. F.,' *Death in a New Dress: or Sportive Funeral Elegies* (London: Isaac Pridmore, 1656); John Taylor, *Odcombs Complaint: or Coriats Funerall Epicedium or Death-Song, Upon his Late Reported Drowning* (London, 1613).

2. William Shakespeare & John Fletcher, *Henry VIII*, prologue, lines 15–18.

3. Robert Hornback, *The English Clown Tradition from the Middle Ages to Shakespeare* (Cambridge: Boydell & Brewer, 2009), 156.

4. Perhaps the clearest example, although now somewhat forgotten, is the American novelist Margaret George's *The Autobiography of Henry VIII, with Notes by His Fool, Will Somers* (New York: St. Martin's Press, 1986). An insightful and well-written piece of fiction, the novel portrays Somer as a wry comic and sharp-eyed witness to all major events of Henry's reign. For a perceptive study of the novel, cf. Kristen Post Walton, "Through the Eyes of a Fool: Henry VIII and Margaret George's 1986 novel *The Autobiography of Henry VIII: With Notes by His Fool, Will Somers*," in *Henry VIII and History*, ed. by Thomas S. Freeman & Thomas Betteridge (London: Routledge, 2012), 261–74.

5. Cf. Graham Seal, "The Robin Hood Principle: Folklore, History, and the Social Bandit," *Journal of Folklore Research*, 46: 1 (2009), 67–89.

6. Peter Thomson, "The True Physiognomy of a Man: Richard Tarlton and His Legend," *Parergon*, 14: 2 (1997), 29–50.

7. Naomi Jacobs, *The Character of Truth: Historical Figures in Contemporary Fiction* (Carbondale: Southern Illinois University Press), 3.

8. Cf. Peter Burke, "The Renaissance, Individualism and the Portrait," *History of European Ideas*, 21: 3 (1995), 393–400; John Jeffries Martin, *Myths of Renaissance Individualism* (New York: St. Martin's Press, 2004); Douglas Biow, *On the Importance of Being an Individual in Renaissance Italy: Men, Their Professions, and Their Beards* (Philadelphia: University of Pennsylvania Press, 2015).

9. Nigel Hamilton, *Biography: A Brief History* (Cambridge, MA: Harvard University Press, 2007), 78–79.

10. Douglas Bruster, "The Structural Transformation of Print in Late Elizabethan England," in *Print Manuscript Performance: The Changing Relations of the Media in Early Modern England*, ed. by Arthur F. Marotti & Michael D. Bristol (Columbus: Ohio State University Press, 2000), 49–89 (51); Samuel Fallon, *Paper Monsters: Persona and Literary Culture in Elizabethan England* (Philadelphia: University of Pennsylvania Press, 2019).

11. John H. Astington, "Will Sommer's Suit: Illustration of Early Modern Performance," *Popular Entertainment Studies*, 2: 1 (2011), 69–78.

12. Martin Wiggins & Catherine Richardson, *British Drama, 1533-1642: A Catalogue. Volume IV: 1598-1602* (Oxford: Oxford University Press, 2014), 307, 346.

13. On the genre of jest biographies, cf. F. P. Wilson, "The English Jestbooks of the Sixteenth and Early Seventeenth Centuries," *Huntington Library Quarterly*, 2: 2 (1939), 121–58.

14. *The first and best part of Scoggins iests full of witty mirth and pleasant shifts* (London: Francis Williams, 1626), 27–28 (first surviving edition, believed to have been written around 1540).

15. George Cavendish, *The Life of Cardinal Wolsey*, ed. by Samuel Weller Singer (London: Thomas Davison, 1827), 237.

16. *A pleasant History Of the Life and Death of Will Summers* (London: J. Okes, 1637), n.p.

17. Richard Beadle, "Crab's Pedigree," in *English Comedy*, ed. by Michael Cordner, Peter Holland, & John Kerrigan (Cambridge: Cambridge University Press, 1994).

18. *A pleasant History*, n.p.

19. On Lean Leanard, cf. Peter Cockett, "Performing Natural Folly: The Jests of Lean Leanard and the Touchstones of Robert Armin and David Tennant," *New Theatre Quarterly*, 22: 2 (2006), 141–54.

20. Thomson, "True Physiognomy of a Man."

21. Timothy R. Tangherlini, "'It Happened Not Too Far from Here . . .': A Survey of Legend Theory and Characterization," *Western Folklore*, 49: 4 (1990), 371–90 (378).

22. Samuel Rowley, *When you see me, you know me* (London: Nathaniell Butter, 1605).

23. Rowley, *When you see me, you know me*, n.p.

24. Teresa Grant, "History in the Making: The Case of Samuel Rowley's *When You See Me You Know Me* (1604/5)," in *English Historical Drama, 1500-1660: Forms outside the Canon*, ed. by Teresa Grant & Barbara Ravelhofer (Basingstoke: Palgrave Macmillan, 2008), 125–57.

25. Joanna Nicole Howe, "A Critical Edition of Samuel Rowley's *When You See Me, You Know Me*," unpublished PhD thesis, Bath Spa University, 2015, 46–47. Howe bases her argument mainly on H. Dugdale Sykes, who first made this attribution in his *Sidelights on Elizabethan Drama* (London: Routledge, 1966).

26. Charles C. Mish, "Will Summers: An Unrecorded Jestbook," *Philological Quarterly*, 31: 2 (1952), 215–18.

27. Cf. Bart Van Es, "His Fellow Actors Will Kemp, Robert Armin and Other Members of the Lord Chamberlain's Men and the King's Men," in *The Shakespeare Circle: An Alternative Biography*, ed. by Paul Edmondson & Stanley Wells (Cambridge: Cambridge University Press, 2015), 261–74.

28. Wes Folkerth, "Reading Shakespeare after Neurodiversity," in *Performing Disability in Early Modern English Drama*, ed. by Leslie C. Dunn (Cham: Springer, 2020), 144.

29. Cf. David Wiles, *Shakespeare's Clown: Actor and Text in the Elizabethan Playhouse* (Cambridge: Cambridge University Press, 1987), 137–43; Van Es, "His Fellow Actors."

30. Robert Armin, *Foole Vpon Foole, or Six Sortes of Sottes* (London: William Ferbrand, 1600), E 2.

31. Armin, *Foole Vpon Foole*.

32. Armin, *Foole Vpon Foole*, F 1.

33. Robert Armin, *A Nest of Ninnies. Simply of themselves without Compound* (London: John Deane, 1608).

34. Cf. Charles Nicholl, *A Cup of News: The Life of Thomas Nashe* (London: Routledge & Kegan Paul, 1984), 135–39; Beatrice Groves, "Laughter in the Time of Plague: A Context for the Unstable Style of Nashe's *Christ's Tears over Jerusalem*," *Studies in Philology*, 108: 2 (2011), 238–60.

35. Nashe, *Unfortunate Traveller*, 147.

36. Nashe, *Unfortunate Traveller*, 192.

37. Nashe, *Unfortunate Traveller*, 181.

38. Mish, "Will Summers."

39. Lester Ernest Barber, "Misogonus: Edited with an Introduction," doctoral dissertation (University of Arizona, 1967), introduction, passim; Wiggins, *British Drama*, vol. 2, 175; G. L. Kittredge, "The 'Misogonus' and Laurence Johnson," *Journal of Germanic Philology*, 3: 3 (1901), 335–41.

40. Barber, "Misogonus," 64.

41. Cf. Wiggins, *British Drama*, vol. 1, 245–48, 266–69.

42. Barber, "Misogonus," 67.

43. Barber, "Misogonus," 102–4.

44. Barber, "Misogonus," 105.

45. Barber, "Misogonus," 106.

46. Barber, "Misogonus," 142.

47. Barber, "Misogonus," 111. See Pauline White, "'Children and Fools, They Say, Cannot Lie': A Proverb Turned Upside Down in Anthony Rudd's *Misogonus*," *Revue LISA*, 6: 3 (2008), 198–206.

48. Barber, "Misogonus," 222.

49. Cf. R. W. Maslen, "The Afterlife of Andrew Borde," *Studies in Philology*, 100: 4 (2003), 463–92.

50. Katherine Duncan-Jones, "The Life, Death and Afterlife of Richard Tarlton," *Review of English Studies*, 65: 268 (2014), 18–32 (19).

51. Duncan-Jones, "Life, Death and Afterlife," 19.

52. Ulpian Fulwell, *The first parte, of the eyghth liberall science: entituled, Ars adulandi, the arte of flatterie* (London: Richard Iones, 1579).

53. Thomas Stapleton, *A returne of vntruthes vpon M. Jewelles replie* (Antwerp: John Latius, 1566), 38.

54. Gabriel Harvey, *Pierces supererogation or A new prayse of the old asse* (London: Iohn Vvolfe, 1593), 75.

55. H. F. Lippincott, "*King Lear* and the Fools of Robert Armin," *Shakespeare Quarterly*, 26: 3 (1975), 243–53.

Chapter Three

1. Paromita Chakravarti, "Natural Fools and the Historiography of Renaissance Folly," *Renaissance Studies*, 25: 2 (2010), 208–27. The works she criticises are, apart from Welsford's aforementioned book, Michel Foucault, *Madness and Civilization: A History of Insanity in the Age of Reason* (New York: Pantheon Books, 1965); Anton C. Zijderveld, *Reality in a Looking-Glass: Rationality through an Analysis of Traditional Folly* (London: Routledge, 1982); George Rosen, *Madness and Society: Chapters in the Historical Sociology of Mental Illness* (London: Routledge, 1968).

2. Cf. Mikhail Bakhtin, *Rabelais and His World* (Cambridge, MA: MIT Press, 1968); Keith Thomas, "The Place of Laughter in Tudor and Stuart England," *TLS*, 21 January 1977; Peter Burke, *Popular Culture in Early Modern Europe* (Farnham, England: Ashgate, 2009).

3. Chakravarti, "Natural Fools," 214.

4. Metzler, *Fools and Idiots*, 174, 84.

5. Metzler, *Fools and Idiots*, 200.

6. Erik Midelfort, *A History of Madness in Sixteenth-Century Germany* (Stanford, CA: Stanford University Press, 1999), 234–35.

7. Midelfort, *History of Madness*, 262, 265, 275–76.

8. Chakravarti, "Natural Fools."

9. Pamela Allen Brown, "Bad Fun and Tudor Laughter," in *A Companion to Tudor Literature*, ed. by Kent Cartwright (Oxford: Blackwell, 2010), 324–38.

10. Anu Korhonen, *Fellows of Infinite Jest: The Fool in Renaissance England* (Turku, Finland: University of Turku, 1999), 301–2.

11. Korhonen, *Fellows of Infinite Jest*, 305.

12. Korhonen, *Fellows of Infinite Jest*, 307.

13. Cf. Peter Happé, "Staging Folly in the Early Sixteenth Century: Heywood, Lindsay, and Others," in *Fools and Folly*, ed. by Clifford Davidson (Kalamazoo, MI: Medieval Institute Publications, 1996), 74, 81.

14. Quoted in Korhonen, *Fellows of Infinite Jest*, 87.

15. Thomas More, *A Frutefull Pleasaunt, and Wittie Worke, of the Beste State of a Publique Weale, and of the Newe Yle, Called Vtopia*, transl. by Raphe Robynson (London: Abraham Vele, 1556), fol. 96v.

16. Sarah Carpenter, "Laughing at Natural Fools," *Theta XI, Théatre Tudor* (2013), 3–22 (15).

17. Billington, *Social History of the Fool*, 27; Southworth, *Fools and Jesters*, 48.

18. Cf. Southworth, *Fools and Jesters*; and Guillaume Berthon, "'Triboulet a frères et soeurs'—Fou de cour et littérature tournant des XVe et XVIe siècles," *Babel. Littératures plurielles*, 25 (2021), 97–120.

19. Metzler, *Fools and Idiots*, 186. She claims that Southworth agrees with this, but in fact he says the opposite: "If the artificial or counterfeit fools are assumed to have modelled their behaviour on genuine madmen or 'simpletons', the precedence of the latter may be taken for granted." Southworth, *Fools and Jesters*, 48.

20. Nadia T. van Pelt, "Katherine of Aragon's Deathbed: Why Chapuys Brought a Fool," *Early Theatre*, 24: 1 (2021), 63–87.

21. Cf. van Pelt, "Katherine of Aragon's Deathbed"; Lenke Kovács, "Frightened or Fearless: Different Ways of Facing Death in the Sixteenth-Century Majorcan Play *Representaci de la Mort*," in *Mixed Metaphors: The Danse Macabre in Medieval and Early Modern Europe*, ed. by Sophie Oosterwijk & Stefanie Knöll (Cambridge: Cambridge Scholars Publishing, 2011), 207–36.; Nikolas Jaspert, "Das aragonesische Dilemma: Die Heimat Benedikts XIII. zwischen Obödienzstreit, herrschaftlichem Umbruch un internationaler Verflechtung," in *Das Konstanzer Konzil als europäisches Ereignis. Begegnungen, Medien und Ritualen*, ed. by Gabriela Signori & Birgit Studt (Ostfildern: Jan Thorbecke Verlag, 2014), 107–41.

22. Francesc Massip Bonet, "El personaje del loco en el espectáculo medieval y en las cortes principescas del renacimiento," *Babel. Littératures plurielles*, 25 (2021), 71–96.

23. Metzler, *Fools and Idiots*, 118–19.

24. Metzler, *Fools and Idiots*, 75–77.

25. Goodey, *History of Intelligence*, 237; Sergey A. Ivanov, *Holy Fools in Byzantium and Beyond* (Oxford: Oxford University Press, 2006), 1.

26. Stephen Greenblatt, *Renaissance Self-Fashioning: From More to Shakespeare* (Chicago: University of Chicago Press 1980), 162.

27. T. J. Clark, "Masters and Fools," *London Review of Books*, 43: 18 (23 September 2021).

28. Clark, "Masters and Fools." Erving Goffman differentiates between "engagement" in a role, wherein the individual embraces the role he or she has been given and "disappear[s] completely into the virtual self available in the situation," and what he terms "role distance"—the act of explicitly or discreetly demonstrating a distance to the role, "denying not the role but the virtual self that is implied in the role for all accepting performers." This requires an audience for it to be pulled off, since one purpose of it is to demonstrate to one's surroundings that one does not belong. Goffman gives the example of children riding a carousel, in which they both think they are a bit too old for it and enjoy it at the same time. He also notes a middle road, in which the individual "affect[s] the embracing of a role in order to conceal a lack of attachment to it." Erving Goffman, *Encounters: Two Studies in the Sociology of Interaction* (Indianapolis: Bobbs-Merrill, 1961), 106–9.

29. JoAnn Cavallo, "Joking Matters: Politics and Dissimulation in Castiglione's *Book of the Courtier*," *Renaissance Quarterly*, 53: 2 (2000), 402–24 (422). See also Jon R. Snyder, *Dissimulation and the Culture of Secrecy in Early Modern Europe* (Berkeley: University of California Press, 2009).

30. Ryan Schmitz, "Sancho's Courtly Performance: *Discreción* and the Art of Conversation in the Ducal Palace Episodes of *Don Quijote II*," *MLN*, 128: 2 (2013), 445–55.

31. Metzler, *Fools and Idiots*, 189–91.

32. Yi-Fu Tuan, *Dominance and Affection: The Making of Pets* (New Haven, CT: Yale University Press, 1984), 154–66. These few pages on court fools contain a number of uncorroborated claims, such as the nature of Madame Rambouillet's household and the assertion that Renaissance courts tried to breed dwarfs.

33. Welsford, *The Fool*, 73–75.

34. Otto, *Fools Are Everywhere*, 244. Curiously, Otto supports her claim by stating that "an informal survey of the man in the street has shown that most people will pinpoint the jester's right to speak his mind as one of his salient characteristics." She gives no reference to any recorded survey, however.

35. See, for instance, Walter Kaiser, *Praisers of Folly: Erasmus, Rabelais, Shakespeare* (Cambridge, MA: Harvard University Press, 1963); H. F. Lippincott, "*King*

Lear and the Fools of Robert Armin," *Shakespeare Quarterly*, 26: 3 (1975), 243–53; Robert Hornback, "The Fool in Quarto and Folio *King Lear*," *English Literary Renaissance*, 34: 3 (2004), 306–38. For an excellent critique of this myth, see Wes Folkerth, "Intellectual Disability and the Fool's License in Shakespeare," in *Shaping Intellectual Disabilities in Early Modern Literature and Culture*, ed. by Alice Equestri, forthcoming.

Chapter Four

1. Armin, *Foole Vpon Foole*, E v.

2. James Granger, *A Biographical History of England, from Egbert the Great to the Revolution*, vol. 1 (London: T. Davies, 1769), 85–86.

3. Granger, *Biographical History of England*, 85–86.

4. On the annals and chronicles of the Benedictines at Teignmouth, cf. Jaime Goodrich, "The Antiquarian and the Abbess: Gender, Genre, and the Reception of Early Modern Historical Writing," *Journal of Medieval and Early Modern Studies*, 50: 1 (2020), 95–113.

5. Quoted in *The Chronicle of the English Augustinian Canonesses Regular of the Lateran, at St Monica's in Louvain. A Continuation, 1625 to 1644*, ed. by Dom Adam Hamilton (London: Sands, 1906), 119–20.

6. I am grateful to Professor Jayme Goodrich for sharing her research on the Teignmouth abbey chronicle with me.

7. J. J. Scarisbrick, "Religion and Politics in Northamptonshire in the Reign of Henry VIII," *Northamptonshire Past and Present*, 5 (1974), 85–90.

8. Cf. Basil Morgan, "Fermor, Richard," *ODNB*.

9. Muriel St. Clare Byrne, ed., *The Lisle Letters, Volume One* (Chicago: University of Chicago Press, 1981), 569.

10. Cf. Susan Brigden, "Thomas Cromwell and the 'Brethren,'" in *Law and Government under the Tudors*, ed. by Claire Cross, David Loades, & J. J. Scarisbrick (Cambridge: Cambridge University Press, 1988), 34. See also *L&P*: December 1527; March 1528, vol. 4; September 1532, vol. 5; March 1533, vol. 6.

11. *L&P*, January 1544, vol. 19, 28–45; *A History of the County of Hampshire*, vol. 3 (London: Victorian County History, 1908), 377; vol. 4, 1911, 210–19; C 142/101/113 (NA).

12. For a case illustrative of this, albeit of a later date, cf. Rab Houston & Uta Frith, *Autism in History: The Case of Hugh Blair of Borgue* (Oxford: Blackwell, 2000).

13. Quoted in L. Gaches, "The Abbot of Crowland's Fool," *Fenland Notes & Queries*, vol. 2 (1894), 284–85 (284).

14. *L&P*, Miscellaneous 1535, vol. 9. Heron is mentioned again in a list of pensions assigned to "the late nuns and lay sisters of the Minories." *L&P*, April 1539, vol. 14, part 1.

15. Eileen Power, *Medieval English Nunneries, c. 1275 to 1535* (Cambridge: Cambridge University Press, 1922), 33.

16. Quoted in Peter Thomson, "Tarlton, Richard," *ODNB*.

17. Maurice Lever, *Le sceptre et la marotte: Histoire des fous de cour* (Paris: Fayard, 1983), 244–45. See also Billington, *Social History of the Fool*, 35–36.

18. *Two Early Tudor Lives*, ed. by Richard S. Sylvester & Davis P. Harding (New Haven, CT: Yale University Press, 1962), 107.

19. Southworth, *Fools and Jesters*, 67.

Chapter Five

1. A verse epitaph on a fool called "Lobbe," described as "the king's fool" but not present in any royal records, has been dated to around 1518. Cf. R. J. Schoeck, "A Fool to Henry VIII at Lincoln's Inn: 'Lobbe, the Kynges Foole,'" *Modern Language Notes*, 66: 8 (1951), 506–9.

2. John Heywood, *John Heywood's Works and Miscellaneous Short Poems*, ed. by Burton A. Milligan (Urbana: University of Illinois Press, 1956), 124.

3. "Henry VIII: Privy Purse Expences," in *Letters and Papers, Foreign and Domestic, Henry VIII, Volume 5, 1531-1532*, ed. by James Gairdner (London: Her Majesty's Stationery Office, 1880), 747–62.

4. *The Privy Purse Expenses of Henry VIII, 1529-1532*, ed. by N. H. Nicolas (London: William Pickering, 1827), 114.

5. *Privy Purse Expenses*, 128, 245.

6. "Henry VIII: Miscellaneous, 1538," in *Letters and Papers, Foreign and Domestic, Henry VIII, Volume 13 Part 2, August-December 1538*, ed. by James Gairdner (London: Her Majesty's Stationery Office, 1893), 496–539.

7. Transcribed in *Archaeologia*, vol. 9, 1789. Somer's name recurs in wardrobe accounts again on 29 September 1539 (LP 14: 2, 67–102).

8. LC 5/31 ff. 75–79. Transcribed in Hilary Doda, "Of Crymsen Tissue: The Construction of a Queen: Identity, Legitimacy and the Wardrobe of Mary Tudor," unpublished MA thesis (Halifax: Dalhousie University, 2011), 181.

9. LC 5/31 ff. 94–99. Transcribed in Doda, "Of Crymsen Tissue," 190.

10. Cf. Robin O'Bryan, "A Tortoise, a Fish, a Jester, and a 'Jesuit': Valerio Cioli's Dwarf Sculptures for the Boboli Gardens," *Source: Notes in the History of Art*, 38: 3 (2019), 133–42.

11. See, for instance, E 101/426/5 (NA).

12. Hilary Mantel, *Wolf Hall* (London: Fourth Estate, 2010), 56–57.

13. *Letters and Papers, Foreign and Domestic, Henry VIII, Volume 21 Part 2, September 1546-January 1547*. Originally published by His Majesty's Stationery Office, London, 1910, pp. 388–453.

14. Hester W. Chapman, *The Last Tudor King: A Study of Edward VI* (London: Jonathan Cape 1958), 243.

15. A "dizzard," spelt various ways, was a synonym of fool or idiot used in the sixteenth and seventeenth centuries.

16. 1 August 1532, in *Letters and Papers, Foreign and Domestic, Henry VIII, Volume 5, 1531-1532*, 531.

17. "Spain: July 1535, 1-31," in *Calendar of State Papers, Spain, Volume 5 Part 1, 1534-1535*, ed. by Pascual de Gayangos (London: Her Majesty's Stationery Office, 1886), 507–23 (520). It is noteworthy that the translation of the French *un innocent* into "a simple, innocent man" alters Chapuys's conception of the fool, whom he portrays as an idiot.

18. Southworth, *Fools and Jesters*, 68–69. Hilary Mantel, incidentally, follows this interpretation and dramatises the incident briefly. Cf. Hilary Mantel, *The Mirror & the Light* (London: Fourth Estate, 2020), 96–97.

19. Weir, *Henry VIII*, 365.

20. "Letters and Papers: Miscellaneous, 1539," in *Letters and Papers, Foreign and Domestic, Henry VIII, Volume 14 Part 2, August-December 1539*, ed. by James Gairdner & R. H. Brodie (London: Her Majesty's Stationery Office, 1895), 303–58.

21. A payment is made for three geese and a hen for Jane Foole in October 1544, suggesting perhaps a pastime or an additional function. LP 19: 2, 396–421. For Browne, see LP 21: 1, 305–34.

22. This picture of the court is primarily based on Retha Warnicke, "The Court," in *A Companion to Tudor Britain*, ed. by Robert Tittler & Norman L. Jones (Malden, MA: Blackwell, 2004), 61–76; David Loades, *Intrigue and Treason: The Tudor Court, 1547-1558* (Harlow, England: Pearson Education, 2004), 1–3, 303–8; Simon Thurley, *Houses of Power: The Places That Shaped the Tudor World* (London: Black Swan, 2019), 213–14.

23. "Ordinances for the Household Made at Eltham," in *A Collection of Or-dinances and Regulations for the Government of the Royal Household, Made in Divers Reigns* (London: Society of Antiquaries, 1790), 201.

24. *The Inventory of King Henry VIII. Society of Antiquaries MS 129 and British Library MS Harley 1419. The Transcript*, ed. by David Starkey (London: Harvey Miller Publishers 1998), 164.

25. Cf. *The Report of the Royal Commission of 1552*, ed. by W. C. Richardson (Morgantown: West Virginia University Library 1974), 114–18.

26. For information on this document, see Dale Hoak, "The Secret History of the Tudor Court: The King's Coffers and the King's Purse, 1542-1553," *Journal of British Studies*, 26: 2 (1987), 208–31.

27. Lansdowne Charter 14 (BL).

28. E 101/426/14 (NA).

29. Cf. Robin O'Bryan, "Grotesque Bodies, Princely Delights: Dwarfs in Italian Renaissance Court Imagery," *Preternature: Critical and Historical Studies on the Preternatural*, 1: 2 (2012), 252–88; Touba Ghadessi, "Lords and Monsters: Visible Emblems of Rule," *I Tatti Studies in the Italian Renaissance*, 16: 1/2 (2013), 491–523.

30. On Ferrers, see Charles Beem, "The Pastimes of George Ferrers: Recon-structing the Life and Career of a Tudor Renaissance Gentleman," *Explorations in Renaissance Culture*, 37: 1 (2011), 157–74.

31. *Documents Relating to the Revels at Court in the Time of King Edward VI and Queen Mary (The Loseley Manuscripts)*, ed. by Albert Feuillerat (Louvain: A. Uystpruyst, 1914), 49.

32. *Documents Relating to the Revels*, 67, 73.

33. Hornback, *English Clown Tradition*, 76–77.

34. Wiles, *Shakespeare's Clown*, 22. Richard Preiss has questioned the Vice as precursor to the clown, seeing instead the Jack-a-Lent figure of carnival as its true origin, but the Vice character was certainly recurrent enough to suggest some importance in the development. Richard Preiss, *Clowning and Authorship in Early Modern Theatre* (Cambridge: Cambridge University Press, 2014), 67–68.

35. Southworth, *Fools and Jesters*, 77.

36. Cf. Stephen Alford, *Edward VI: The Last Boy King* (London: Penguin, 2018), 57–60.

37. There is a line break after his name, but considering the relative conse-quence in not ending his name with *s* in contemporary records, I take this to be

a genitive case. The line break occurs at the very edge of the paper, so it must have been by necessity.

38. The two papers are catalogued as SP 46/1/fo122 and SP 46/1/fo123 at the NA.

39. Will Fisher, "The Renaissance Beard: Masculinity in Early Modern England," *Renaissance Quarterly*, 54: 1 (2001), 155–87; Eleanor Rycroft, *Facial Hair and the Performance of Early Modern Masculinity* (London: Routledge, 2019).

40. Transcriptions in C. C. Stopes, "Jane, the Queen's Fool," *The Athenaeum*, 4059 (August 1905), 200–220.

41. Transcriptions from Doda, "Of Crymsen Tissue," 169, 179, 191, 199. Only wardrobe accounts from the years 1554, 1557, and 1558 exist. For details, cf. Alison J. Carter, "Mary Tudor's Wardrobe," *Costume*, 18: 1 (1984), 9–28. Carter excludes the fools from her transcripts of the accounts, however.

42. Doda, "Of Crymsen Tissue," 188.

43. Cf. Natasha Awais-Dean, *Bejewelled: Men and Jewellery in Tudor and Jacobean England* (London: British Museum, 2017).

44. Anu Korhonen, "How to Read a Renaissance Fool," in *Making Sense as a Cultural Practice: Historical Perspectives* (Bielefeld, Germany: Transcript Verlag, 2013), 168–69.

45. *An Edition of Robert Wilson's Three Ladies of London and Three Lords and Three Ladies of London*, ed. by H. S. D. Mithal (London: Garland, 1988), 106.

Chapter Six

1. Lipscomb, "All the King's Fools"; Southworth, *Fools and Jesters*, 74.

2. See Cockett, "Performing Natural Folly," 144; Jessie Childs, *Henry VIII's Last Victim: The Life and Times of Henry Howard, Earl of Surrey* (London: Vintage, 2008) 98; Andrew McConnell Stott, "'Let Them Use Their Talents': *Twelfth Night* and the Professional Comedian," in *Twelfth Night: A Critical Reader*, ed. by Alison Findlay & Liz Oakley-Brown (London: Bloomsbury, 2014), 134; Mantel, *Mirror & the Light*, 275.

3. Reproduced in Roy Strong, *Tudor & Jacobean Portraits* (London: National Portrait Gallery, 1969).

4. John Husee to Lady Lisle, 21 June 1535, in *Lisle Letters*, vol. 2, 532; John Bishop of Lincoln to Cromwell, 8 July 1534. "Henry VIII: July 1534, 6-10," in *Letters and Papers, Foreign and Domestic, Henry VIII, Volume 7, 1534*, 363–73.

5. Alonso Sánchez Coello, "Infanta Isabel Clara Eugenia and Magdalena Ruiz," 1585-1588, Museo del Prado. The frescoes at Trento are by Girolamo Romanino.

6. If the gardens that Somer and Jane are standing in are the same space, then it could also be considered that he is bowing to her, thus showing his own foolishness by bowing gracefully to another fool, who doesn't even notice him.

7. Ruth Ahnert, "The Psalms and the English Reformation," *Renaissance Studies*, 29: 4 (2015), 493–508.

8. Tracy Borman & Alison Weir, "Elizabeth I: What Does This Forgotten Picture Tell Us about Her?," *BBC History Magazine*, June 2008.

9. See, for instance, Johannes Stradanus, *Engagement of Cosimo and Eleonora's Daughter*, c. 1557, fresco, Palazzo Vecchio, Florence; Juan Bautista Martinez del Mazo, *Queen Mariana of Spain in Mourning*, 1666, National Gallery, London; Diego Velazquez, *Las Meninas*, 1656, Prado, Madrid; Daniel Mytens, *Charles I and Henrietta Maria Departing for the Chase*, c. 1630, Royal Collection, UK.

10. Pamela Allen Brown, "The Mirror and the Cage: Queens and Dwarfs at the Early Modern Court," in *Historical Affects and the Early Modern Theater*, ed. by Ronda Arab, Michelle Dowd, & Adam Zucker (New York: Routledge, 2015).

11. Astington, "Will Sommer's Suit."

12. Mulryne, "Somer, William"; Wiles, *Shakespeare's Clown*, 183.

13. Southworth, *Fools and Jesters*, 77.

14. Alison Weir claims in several texts that he wears a skull cap in the portrait with Mary, but this is obviously a misreading based on looking at a bad photo of the painting.

15. Korhonen, "How to Read a Renaissance Fool," 171.

16. Martin W. Walsh points out that medieval fools' heads were habitually shaven, sometimes in the style of a friar's tonsure, sometimes in more fanciful ways, including a checkerboard pattern. Walsh, "The King His Own Fool: *Robert of Cicyle*," in *Fools and Folly*, ed. by Clifford Davidson (Kalamazoo, MI: Medieval Institute Publications, 1996), 36.

17. Quoted in *Calendar of Charters and Rolls Preserved in the Bodleian Library*, ed. by William H. Turner (Oxford: Clarendon Press, 1878), xviii–xix. Southworth has even conjectured that the clothes Somer is wearing in the psalter illumination are the ones found in an entry in the wardrobe accounts in 1535. A few discrepancies in the details, as well as the generally accepted later date of the psalter, might undermine this, however.

18. Maria Hayward, "Crimson, Scarlet, Murrey and Carnation: Red at the Court of Henry VIII," *Textile History*, 38: 2 (2007), 135–150 (139).

19. There is a payment for a "velvet purse for W. Sommer" in the household expenses of the king in 1538. "Letters and Papers: Miscellaneous, 1539," in *Letters and Papers, Foreign and Domestic, Henry VIII, Volume 14 Part 2, August-December 1539*, 303–58.

20. Wiles, *Shakespeare's Clown*, 183–84.

21. Cf. the portraits of the fools Gonnella in fifteenth-century Ferrara by Jean Fouquet; Jost Amman's "Gesellen-Stechen der bürgerlichen Patrizier-Söhne Nürnbergs, vom 3. März 1561"; the double portrait of Tom Derry and Muckle John known as "We Three Loggerheads," a seventeenth-century painting now in the possession of the Shakespeare Birthplace Trust; and the seventeenth-century portrait of Thomas Skelton, fool at Muncaster Castle. E. W. Ives, "Tom Skelton—a Seventeenth-Century Jester," *Shakespeare Survey*, vol. 13 (1960), 90–105. See also Korhonen, "How to Read a Renaissance Fool," 167.

22. Reproductions of portraits of the first three may be found in E. Tietze-Conrat, *Dwarfs and Jesters in Art* (London: Phaidon Press, 1957). A portrait of Perejón by Anthonis Mor (c. 1560) is in the Prado Museum in Madrid.

23. Jennifer Rae McDermott, "'There's Magic in the Web of It': Skin, Mind and Webs of Touch in Othello," in *Embodied Cognition and Shakespeare's Theatre: The Early Modern Mind-Body*, ed. by Laurie Johnson, John Sutton, & Evelyn Tribble (London: Routledge, 2004), 154–72 (161). See also Michel Pastoureau, *Green: The History of a Colour* (Princeton, NJ: Princeton University Press, 2014), 111; Liz Oakley-Brown, "Robin Hood's Passions: Emotion and Embodiment in Anthony Munday's *The Death of Robert, Earle of Huntington* (c. 1598)," in *Robin Hood and the Outlaw/ed Literary Canon*, ed. by Lesley Coote & Alexander L. Kaufman (New York: Routledge, 2018).

24. Harriet Phillips, *Nostalgia in Print and Performance, 1510-1613: Merry Worlds* (Cambridge: Cambridge University Press, 2019), 140–43, 150; David Wiles, *The Early Plays of Robin Hood* (Cambridge: D. S. Brewer, 1981), 13.

25. Javier Portús, *Velazquez* (Vienna: Kunsthistorisches Museum, 2014), 310–11.

26. Leslie Hotson, *Shakespeare's Motley* (Oxford: Oxford University Press, 1952), 39–46.

27. Erika T. Lin, "Popular Festivity and the Early Modern Stage: The Case of *George a Greene*," *Theatre Journal*, 61: 2 (2009), 271–297 (293).

28. See Dosso Dossi's portrait of an unnamed jester (c. 1510), Hans Mielich's portrait of Bavarian fool Mertl (1545), or David Ehrenstrahl's portrait of Swedish jester Hasenberger (1651).

29. Walsh remarks on the emphatic rusticity of the medieval fool's clothing and how it was meant to resemble the dress of a peasant. Walsh, "The King His Own Fool," 37.

Chapter Seven

1. Peter Happé bases his dating of it on the fact that Will Somer "arrived at court in 1525," but this is pure conjecture, and in his and Richard Axton's edition of Heywood's plays, Somer is quite speedily dealt with, described in a note as an artificial fool, essentially reproducing the notes on Somer found in Fairholt's and Farmer's editions a century earlier. Happé claims to base his dating on stylistic elements, while Greg Walker, in his extensive biography of Heywood, sees a connection between the work's patient and meditative disputational structure and the "relatively stable political and religious climate of the 1520s," whereas the later added last stanzas (see below) suggest the more tumultuous religious debates of the following decade. *Two Moral Interludes*, ed. by Peter Happé, Malone Society Reprints (Oxford: Oxford University Press, 1991), 14; John Heywood, *The Plays of John Heywood*, ed. by Richard Axton & Peter Happé (Cambridge: D. S. Brewer, 1991), 34, 219; Greg Walker, *John Heywood: Comedy and Survival in Tudor England* (Oxford: Oxford University Press, 2020), 19. For Fairholt and Farmer, see note 7 below.

2. Heywood, *Plays*, 56–57.

3. Allen Brown, "Bad Fun and Tudor Laughter."

4. Heywood, *Plays*, 68.

5. Heywood, *Plays*, 68.

6. The word is written as "flak" in Fairholt's and Farmer's editions but spelled "flocke" in Peter Happé's faithful transcription of the original manuscript in the 1991 Malone Society edition. Cf. Happé, *Two Moral Interludes*, 40.

7. John Heywood, *A Dialogue on Wit and Folly*, ed. by F. W. Fairholt (London: Percy Society, 1846), 29–30; John Heywood, *The Dramatic Writings of John Heywood*, ed. by John Farmer (London: Early English Drama Society, 1905), 266–67. Katrina Spadaro also suggests that Heywood's performance as fool in his later interlude *Play of the Wether* was a further attempt to displace Somer. Katrina L.

Spadaro, "Reading Tudor Folly: Sex and Scatology in John Heywood's *Play of the Wether*," *Modern Philology*, 118: 4 (2021), 470–91 (484).

8. Heywood, *Plays*, 73.

9. Jeanne H. McCarthy, "The Emergence of Henrician Drama 'in the Kynges absens,'" *English Literary Renaissance*, 39: 2 (2009), 231–66.

10. Happé, "Staging Folly," 80–81.

11. Cf. Peter Happé, "Heywood, John," *ODNB*.

12. Armin, *Foole Vpon Foole*, E 2.

13. Mantel, *Mirror & the Light*, 275. Her interpretation of the appointed keeper's function to prevent accidents when Somer falls asleep on the town is fanciful but not unappealing—a sign of her meticulous research, if nothing else.

14. Cf. Roy Battenhouse, "Falstaff as Parodist and Perhaps Holy Fool," *PMLA*, 90: 1 (1975), 32–52.

15. Hornback, *English Clown Tradition*, 35; Chris Ritchie, "'Who Do You Think You Are Kidding . . . ?' German Comedy from the Tenth to the Nineteenth Centuries," *Comedy Studies*, 5: 2 (2014), 155–64 (158).

16. *Henry IV, Part 2*, act 1, scene 2, lines 401–2; Goodey, *History of Intelligence*, 227; Metzler, *Fools and Idiots*, 56.

17. Korhonen, *Fellows of Infinite Jest*, 30.

18. Metzler, *Fools and Idiots*, 76–77, 174–75, 191; Korhonen, *Fellows of Infinite Jest*, 87–89.

19. Cf. D. J. Gifford, "Iconographical Notes towards a Definition of the Medieval Fool," *Journal of the Warburg and Courtauld Institutes*, 37: 1 (1974), 336–42.

20. *The courtyer of Count Baldessar Castilio diuided into foure bookes* (London: William Seres, 1561), n.p.

21. On the spread of Castiglione in Tudor England, see Mary Partridge, "Thomas Hoby's English Translation of Castiglione's *Book of the Courtier*," *Historical Journal*, 50: 4 (2007), 769–86.

22. Cf. Hans Rudolf Velten, "Komische Körper: Zur Funktion von Hofnarren und zur Dramaturgie des Lachens im Spätmittelalter," *Zeitschrift für Germanistik*, 11: 2 (2001), 292–317 (311).

23. Roger Ascham, *Toxophilvs the schole of shootinge conteyned in tvvo bookes* (London: Edward Whitchurch, 1545), n.p.

24. Brian Melbancke, *Philotimus. The warre betwixt nature and fortune* (London: Roger Warde, 1583), 77.

25. Thomas Lodge, *An alarum against vsurers* (London: Sampson Clarke, 1584); *Orlando Furioso in English Heroical Verse, by Iohn Haringtō* (London: Richard Field, 1591). A promising reference to "master Somer's chamber" in a letter by Ascham of 1549 most likely indicates Edward Seymour, Duke of Somerset, sometimes abbreviated Somer. Roger Ascham, *The Whole Works of Roger Ascham*, vol. 1, part 1, ed. by J. A. Giles (London: John Russell Smith, 1864), 168.

26. Harvey, *Pierces supererogation*, 75.

27. *A pleasant History*, n.p.

28. Armin, *Foole Vpon Foole*, C4v.

29. Cf. Karen Adkins, *Gossip, Epistemology, and Power: Knowledge Underground* (Basingstoke: Palgrave Macmillan, 2017), 64–66.

30. See Cathy Shrank, "The Bow and the Book: Ascham's *Toxophilus*," in *Roger Ascham and His Sixteenth-Century World*, ed. by Lucy R. Nicholas & Ceri Law (Leiden: Brill, 2021).

31. John Bale, *An expostulation of complaynte agaynste the blasphemyes of a frantick papyst of Hampshire* (London: Ihon Daye, 1552), C1v.

32. Cf. Peter K. Andersson, "'Jag är en riktig människa.' Bygdeoriginal och avvikare mellan stad och landsbygd i det sena 1800-talets Sydsverige," *Scandia*, 81: 1 (2015), 11–39.

33. Hornback, *English Clown Tradition*, 10–12.

34. Cf. Walsh, "The King His Own Fool," 37–38.

Chapter Eight

1. Thomas Wilson, *The Arte of Rhetorique, for the vse of all suche as are studious of Eloquence, sette forth in English* (London: Richard Grafton, 1553), fol. 107.

2. Most writers who quote this comment use it as an example of Somer's wit. See, for instance, Southworth, *Fools and Jesters*, 72; van Pelt, "Katherine of Aragon's Deathbed," 68.

3. I am grateful to Professor Greg Walker for suggesting this meaning to me.

4. The full title of the handwritten poem is "A thvndring answer fallen owt of the lightning skies at the pityfull peticion at the Renowmed Rhetoricien willm Somer, vnto the vnswer sottishe booke of the famous foole Nalinghurst," and it seems to have been occasioned by a book by this Nalinghurst which evidently slanders Somer. Unfortunately, the fool Nalinghurst has not been identified and the poem contains no information on Somer, apart from the indication that he was unable or unwilling to defend himself. Merrill Goldwyn has

conjectured that the poem might be related to Churchyard's enmity with Thomas Nashe, who, as we have seen, was not averse to referring to Somer in his writings. Merrill Harvey Goldwyn, "Some Unpublished Manuscripts by Thomas Churchyard," *Studies in Philology*, 64: 2 (1967), 147–58.

5. Wayne A. Rebhorn, "Baldesar Castiglione, Thomas Wilson, and the Courtly Body of Renaissance Rhetoric," *Rhetorica*, 11: 3 (1993), 241–74 (272).

6. Wilson, *Arte of Rhetorique*, fol. 86v.

7. Thomas Wilson, *The Rule of Reason, conteinyng the Arte of Logique* (London: Richard Grafton, 1553), fol. 65v.

8. Wilson, *Rule of Reason*, fol. 65v.

9. Megan Herrold, "Form," in *A Cultural History of Comedy in the Early Modern Age*, ed. by Andrew McConnell Stott (London: Bloomsbury, 2020), 33.

10. L. E. Whatmore, "William Somers, Henry VIII's Jester," *British Catholic History*, 1: 2 (1951), 128–30. "Quod hic manifestissimum fuit dú delirus quidam qui à natiuitate rationis usu priuatus fuit, Guilelmus Sommer nomine, per uniuersam aulam cursitar magna vocis contentione in hec verba prorumpens, simplicitas unius mendicantis frangit superbiam Regis. Ex ore infantium et lactentium laudem suam perficit Deus, nouo et singulari exemplo ex fatui or suam voluit hic laudem Deus perficere." Thomas Bourchier, *Historia Ecclesiastica de Martyrio Fratrum Ordinis Divi Francisci* (Paris: Jean Poupy, 1582), 22.

11. Cf. Leticia Álvarez-Recio, *Fighting the Antichrist: A Cultural History of Anti-Catholicism in Tudor England* (Eastbourne, UK: Sussex Academic Press, 2018).

12. Rudolf Gwalther, *Antichrist, That is to Saye: A true reporte, that Antichriste is come wher he was borne, of his persone, miracles, what tooles he worketh withall, and what shalbe his ende* (Emden, Germany: Christopher Trutheall, 1556), 146.

13. Proverbs expressing similarity have circulated since the Middle Ages, including "Like will to like," "Birds of a feather flock together," "Like people, like priest," and so on. Cf. *Oxford Dictionary of Proverbs*, ed. by Jennifer Speake (Oxford: Oxford University Press, 2015).

14. Cf. Welsford, *The Fool*, 105, 114; Midelfort, *History of Madness*, 259.

15. Cf. Luisa Rubini Messerli, "The Death of the Royal Dwarf: Mari-Barbóla in Velázquez's Las Meninas," in *Erzählkultur. Beiträge zur kulturwissenschaftlichen Erzählforschung*, ed. by Rolf Wilhelm Brednich (Berlin: Walter de Gruyter, 2009), 327–52.

16. *State Papers Published under the Authority of Her Majesty's Commission, Volume X. King Henry the Eighth, Part V—Continued. Foreign Correspondence, 1544-1545* (London: George E. Eyre & William Spottiswoode, 1849), 782.

17. Welsford, *The Fool*, 166; Southworth, *Fools and Jesters*, 72.

18. John Proctor, *The fal of the late Arrian* (London: William Powell, 1549), n.p.

19. Alan Bryson, "Order and Disorder: John Proctor's *History of Wyatt's Rebellion* (1554)," in *The Oxford Handbook of Tudor Literature, 1485-1603*, ed. by Mike Pincombe & Cathy Shrank (Oxford: Oxford University Press, 2009), 325.

20. Quoted in Patrick Fraser Tytler, *England under the Reigns of Edward VI. and Mary*, vol. II (London: Richard Bentley, 1839), 283–84.

21. Southworth uses the passages from both Paget and Wotton to illustrate Somer's eccentric wit; in Paget's case he reads the entire sentence as a quote from Somer, and in Wotton's case he unfortunately relies on the report of the letter in the *Calendar of State Papers*, which is a summary of the actual letter that alters most of the wording.

22. John Bridges, *The Supremacie of Christian Princes ouer all persons throughout their dominions* (London: Henrie Bynneman, 1573), 199.

23. Quoted by Arthur Sheekman in his introduction to Groucho Marx, *The Groucho Letters: Letters from and to Groucho Marx* (New York: Simon & Schuster, 1967), 8.

24. *Qvestions of Profitable and Pleasant Concernings, Talked of by Two Olde Seniors* (London: Richard Field, 1594), 34.

25. Walker, *John Heywood*, 280.

26. R. Malcolm Smuts, "Armstrong, Archibald," *ODNB*.

27. Andrea Shannon, "'Uncouth Language to a Princes Ears': Archibald Armstrong, Court Jester, and Early Stuart Politics," *Sixteenth Century Journal*, 42: 1 (2011), 99–112.

28. Thomas Harding, *A confutation of a booke intituled An apologie of the Church of England* (Antwerp: Ihon Laet, 1565), 262.

29. There is a similar passage in a book by another exiled priest, John Rastell, also in criticising John Jewel's use of "if": "I confesse vnto you: I can not tel what to saye to such What thens? and What yfs? But if you haue any arte in iudging of them: I pray you, if the skye should fal, were not many larkes like to be taken? And if such kindes of What yfs? as you haue put, might be folowed in other examples: were not manie fooles like to be made and preferred by it, and many Wyll Sommers would they not be found in England, which would quickly saie: what if all the Councell be vnlearned? And what if poore knaues haue as great a gift of wisedome, and knowledge, as the Noble and Learned of the world? Thus far concerning this matter." John Rastell, *A briefe shevve of the false vvares packt together in the named* (Leuven: Apud Ioannem Foulerum, 1567), fol. 126r.

30. Nicolas Kies, "Retrouver la culture dans la nature: Les bon mots involontaires dans la littérature facétieuse de la renaissance," *Seizième Siecle*, 7 (2011), 225–41 (229). A comparative contemporary phenomenon might be the rhetorical strategy of *parrhesia*, in which performative speech was undermined by plain and honest speaking, something that might have fed the vogue for fools. Cf. Pascale Drouet, *Shakespeare and the Denial of Territory: Banishment, Abuse of Power and Strategies of Resistance* (Manchester: Manchester University Press, 2021), 26–27. I am grateful to the anonymous reviewer who drew my attention to this parallel.

31. Cf. Kies, "Retrouver la culture," 229.

32. Cf. Rebhorn, "Castiglione, Wilson, and the Courtly Body," 266.

33. Castiglione, *The courtyer*, n.p.

34. Erasmus, *Praise of Folly* (London: Penguin, 1971), 176.

35. John Heywood, *A fourth hundred of Epygrams, Newly inuented and made by Iohn Heywood* (London: Thomas Berthelettes, 1560), no. 81.

Chapter Nine

1. On the role of space and place in Renaissance foolery, cf. Sarah Carpenter, "The Places of Foolery: Robert Armin and Fooling in Edinburgh," *Medieval English Theatre 37: 'The Best Pairt of Our Play': Essays Presented to John J. McGavin, Part 1*, ed. by Sarah Carpenter, Pamela M. King, Meg Twycross, & Greg Walker (Cambridge: D. S. Brewer, 2015).

2. The burial record is from the church of St. Leonard, Shoreditch, ref. P91/LEN/A/012/MS07499/001 (LMA). The entry reads, "Willm Somers was buried the xvth daye of June," and a manicule drawn in the margin indicates that this is a noteworthy entry. The last court record mentioning Somer concerns the ordering of clothes for him to wear at the coronation of Elizabeth I. Here, he and the aforementioned Jane are referred to as "The quenes Fooles." Cf. Janet Arnold, "The 'Coronation' Portrait of Queen Elizabeth I," *The Burlington Magazine*, 120: 908 (1978), 727–41 (736).

3. C 1/1461/22 (NA).

4. Cf. Philip C. Almond, *Demonic Possessions and Exorcism in Early Modern England: Contemporary Texts and Their Cultural Contexts* (Cambridge: Cambridge University Press, 2004), 240–86.

5. Carpenter, "Places of Foolery," 11, 12. See also Folkerth, "Reading Shakespeare after Neurodiversity." In an article responding to Carpenter's, John J.

McGavin is more sceptical of Armin. Cf. "Close Kin to a Clean Fool: Robert Armin's Account of Jack Miller," *Theta XII—Théâtre Tudor* (2016), 29–56 (45).

6. Molly Clark, "Folly and Improvised Rhyme in *King Lear*," *Review of English Studies*, 72: 306 (2021), 686–706.

7. Cf. *Tudor Verse Satire*, ed. by K. W. Gransden (London: Athlone, 1970), 11.

8. Thomas Stapleton, *The Life and Illustrious Martyrdom of Sir Thomas More*, transl. by Philip E. Hallett, ed. by Katherine Stearns & Emma Curtis (Dallas: CTMS Publishers, 2020), 52.

9. Noeline Hall, "Henry Patenson—Sir Thomas More's Fool," *Moreana*, 27: 101–2 (1990), 75–86 (82).

10. Ellis Heywood, *Il Moro: Ellis Heywood's Dialogue in Memory of Thomas More*, ed. and transl. by Roger Lee Deakins (Cambridge, MA: Harvard University Press, 1972), 20.

11. John Heywood, *John Heywood's Works and Miscellaneous Short Poems*, ed. by Burton A. Milligan (Urbana: University of Illinois Press, 1956), 135.

12. Mark Robson, "Translatio Mori: Ellis Heywood's 'Thomas More,'" *Travels and Translations in the Sixteenth Century: Selected Papers from the Second International Conference of the Tudor Symposium*, ed. by Mike Pincombe (London: Routledge, 2017). Thomas Cromwell also allegedly employed a fool, whose name was Anthony. Cf. Tracy Borman, *Thomas Cromwell: The Untold Story of Henry VIII's Most Faithful Servant* (London: Hodder, 2015), 182.

13. Olga Anna Duhl, "Pace, John," *ODNB*.

14. Peter K. Andersson, "Absolute Monarcho: A Megalomaniac Jester at the Court of Queen Bess," *TLS*, no. 6159, 16 April 2021.

15. This might be compared with the aforementioned observation of Peter Burke that comedy was at this time often seen from the perspective of the joker rather than the victim. See chapter 3.

16. Baldesar Castiglione, *The Book of the Courtier*, transl. by Charles Singleton, ed. by Daniel Javitch (New York: Norton, 2002), 43.

17. The appreciation of authenticity later fed into Elizabethan comedy and the mocking portrayal of characters who try too hard to be what they are not. Cf. Alexander Leggatt, *English Stage Comedy, 1490-1990: Five Centuries of a Genre* (London: Routledge, 1998), 41.

18. Indira Ghose, *Shakespeare and Laughter: A Cultural History* (Manchester: Manchester University Press, 2008).

19. Cf. Norbert Elias, *The Court Society* (Oxford: Blackwell, 1983).

20. Cf. Indira Ghose, "Laughter," in Stott, *A Cultural History of Comedy in the Early Modern Age*, 182.

21. Happé, "Staging Folly." On the role of fools in France in connection with the genre of the *sottie*, cf. Lia B. Ross, "You Had to Be There: The Elusive Humor of the *Sottie*," in *Laughter in the Middle Ages and Early Modern Times: Epistemology of a Fundamental Human Behavior, Its Meaning, and Consequences*, ed. by Albrecht Classen & Marilyn Sandidge (Berlin: De Gruyter, 2018).

22. Cf. Silvio A. Bedini, *The Pope's Elephant* (Manchester: Carcanet, 1997), 90–100.

23. Emily Lathrop, in her recent survey of Renaissance attitudes toward intellectual disability, emphasises how foolishness was associated with the lower classes, "particularly those outside of urban spaces." Emily Lathrop, "Learning Difficulties: The Idiot and the Outsider in the Renaissance," in Anderson & Haydon, *Cultural History of Disability*, 142.

24. Cf. Adam Fox, *Oral and Literate Culture in England, 1500-1700* (Oxford: Clarendon Press, 2000).

25. Peter Burke, "Civil Tongue: Language and Politeness in Early Modern Europe," in *Civil Histories: Essays Presented to Sir Keith Thomas*, ed. by Peter Burke, Brian Harrison, & Paul Slack (Oxford: Oxford University Press, 2000); Laura Gowing, *Domestic Dangers: Women, Words and Sex in Early Modern London* (Oxford: Clarendon Press, 1996), 59–67; *The Spoken Word: Oral Culture in Britain, 1500-1850*, ed. by Adam Fox & Daniel Woolf (Manchester: Manchester University Press, 2002).

26. Greenblatt, *Renaissance Self-Fashioning*. See also Peter Burke, *The Art of Conversation* (Cambridge: Polity Press, 1993), 68.

27. Citing psychologist Roger Smith, Christopher Goodey has pointed out that, in history, intellectual deficiency is often indistinguishable from a lack of inhibition, which he connects to the outspokenness of court jesters. Goodey, *History of Intelligence*, 237.

28. Dorinda Outram makes a similar point in her *Four Fools in the Age of Reason*, 127.

29. Korhonen, *Fellows of Infinite Jest*, 305.

Chapter Ten

1. Woody Allen, *Everything You Always Wanted to Know about Sex* (*But Were Afraid to Ask)* (United Artists, 1972).

2. This phrasing is in the first quarto edition, scene 9, lines 19–21. Cf. *The First Quarto of Hamlet*, ed. by Kathleen O. Irace (Cambridge: Cambridge University Press, 1998), 67.

3. Oliver Double, *Getting the Joke: The Inner Workings of Stand-Up Comedy* (London: Bloomsbury, 2014), 113–14; Sarah Balkin, "Theory: Deadpan and Comic Theory," in *A Cultural History of Comedy in the Age of Empire*, ed. by Matthew Kaiser (London: Bloomsbury, 2020), 43–66.

4. In turn, Bart Van Es, "Pedlar of Print: Robert Armin and the Fool's Part in Shakespeare," *TLS*, 25 January 2013; Steve Sohmer, *Reading Shakespeare's Mind* (Manchester: Manchester University Press, 2017), 93; Molly Clark, "Folly and Improvised Rhyme in *King Lear*."

5. On the fear of fakes, cf. Metzler, *Fools and Idiots*, 185; Billington, *Social History of the Fool*, 20.

6. Wiles, *Shakespeare's Clown*, x.

7. John Florio, *A VVorlde of Vvordes, or Most Copious and Exact Dictionarie in Italian and English* (London: Edward Blount, 1598).

8. William Rankins, *A Mirrour of Monsters* (London: Thomas Hacket, 1587), 7.

9. Anthony Copley, *Wits Fittes and Fancies. Fronted and Entermedled with Presidentes of Honour and Wisdome* (London: Richard Iohnes, 1595).

10. Preiss, *Clowning and Authorship*, 201.

11. Cf. Hornback, *English Clown Tradition*, 151–52.

12. Cf. John Kerrigan, "Revision, Adaptation, and the Fool of *King Lear*," in *The Division of the Kingdoms: Shakespeare's Two Versions of King Lear*, ed. by Gary Taylor & Michael Warren (Oxford: Clarendon Press, 1983), 195–239 (218).

13. Hornback, *English Clown Tradition*, 183–86.

14. *Love's Labour's Lost*, act 4, scene 3, line 15.

15. On Cox, cf. Mary Chan, "Drolls, Drolleries and Mid-seventeenth-century Dramatic Music in England," *Royal Musical Association Research Chronicle*, 15 (1979), 117–73 (117–18); Bernard Capp, *England's Culture Wars: Puritan Reformation and Its Enemies in the Interregnum, 1649-1660* (Oxford: Oxford University Press, 2012), 197.

16. Ives, "Tom Skelton." On Black John, cf. "Black John," *All the Year Round*, 3 June 1865, 454–56.

17. A portrait of Kopperman dated circa 1740 hangs at Hampton Court Palace.

18. Cf. Sünne Juterczenka, "'Chamber Moors' and Court Physicians: On the Convergence of Aesthetic Consumption and Racial Anthropology at Eighteenth-Century Courts in Germany," in *Entangled Knowledge: Scientific Discourse and Cultural Difference*, ed. by Klaus Hock & Gesa Mackenthun (Münster: Waxmann, 2012), 165–82.

19. The stereotypical comic woman has a different pedigree. Emerging from commedia dell'arte, she is the scheming maid who is angry and tired of the patriarchy and seeks revenge by tricking men. Cf. Peter K. Andersson, *Komikerns historia* [The history of the comedian] (Stockholm: Natur & Kultur, 2020), 107–19.

20. Welsford, *The Fool*, 318.

21. Quoted in Andrew Stott, *Comedy* (London: Routledge, 2014), 1.

Index